PUBLIC EDUCATION UNDER SCRUTINY

Richard M. Brandt

UNIVERSITY
PRESS OF
AMERICA

LANHAM • NEW YORK • LONDON

Copyright © 1981 by

Richard M. Brandt

University Press of America," Inc.

4720 Boston Way
Lanham, MD 20706

3 Henrietta Street
London WC2E 8LU England

Printed in the United States of America

ISBN (Perfect): 0-8191-3096-6
ISBN (Cloth): 0-8191-3095-8

Library of Congress Cataloging in Publication Data
Brandt, Richard Martin, 1922–
    Public education under scrutiny.

    Bibliography: p.
    1. Public schools–United States. I. Title.
LA217.B73   371'.01'0973   80–6080
ISBN 0–8191–1566–5   AACR2
ISBN 0–8191–1567–3 (pbk.)

TABLE OF CONTENTS

This book is dedicated to the hundreds of thousands of parents and citizens who, as school board members, parent-teacher organization leaders, classroom aides, and citizen volunteers, give freely of their time and talent every year to the service of public education.

ABBREVIATIONS

ACT	—	American College Testing Program
CETA	—	Comprehensive Employment and Training Act
ESEA	—	Elementary and Secondary Education Act
ETS	—	Education Testing Service
GNP	—	gross national product
NAEP	—	National Assessment of Educational Progress
NCES	—	National Center for Education Statistics
NEA	—	National Education Association
NIE	—	National Institute of Education
NIH		National Institute of Health
R & D	—	research and development
SAT	—	Scholastic Aptitude Test
SEA	—	State Education Agency
SES	—	socioeconomic status
SRI	—	Stanford Research Institute
USDE	—	United States Department of Education
USOE	—	United States Office of Education
YETP	—	Youth Employment Training Program

PREFACE AND ACKNOWLEDGEMENTS

During the past decade, grave doubts have been raised about the effectiveness of our system of public education. Declining test results have made front-page news. Teacher strikes have become commonplace, and the busing controversy remains unresolved. Letters to the editor complain about a lack of school discipline, the high crime rate in schools, illiterate high school graduates, and even illiterate teachers. Education, seemingly, is in disarray.

From this period of doubt and controversy should emerge a system of education considerably different from the one we have known this past half-century. Compared with today's schools, those of the future will likely offer parents and pupils (a) many more alternatives of what is to be studied and how it is to be taught, and (b) greater involvement in all aspects of school policy-making and operations. Through the use of new technology and greater differentiation of teaching roles, instruction will be tailored more closely than ever to pupils' learning needs and capabilities. As they become increasingly effective and articulate about their successes, teachers will achieve dignity and recognition as true professionals.

Reassessments of what schools should and should not be expected to do will not restrict what is taught to the "basics" alone; they will force greater attention to areas of cognitive development which schools are singularly equipped to influence and less concern about broad social problems with which other institutions also deal. Schools have had to carry more than their fair share of responsibility for desegregating society, eliminating prejudice, and reducing the disastrous effects of poverty.

Along with teaching and curriculum changes will come improved formulas for financing education. Local property taxes will gradually carry less of the total burden and state and federal taxes more. Despite the usual tendencies for power to follow the "buck," this shift in funding can and should occur under reduced bureaucratic control at the state and, particularly, federal levels. Increased use of simple formula funding and elimination of wasteful, ineffective, categorical aid programs would go a long way toward returning control to local citizens where it belongs.

It is far from certain that all these good things will come to pass. The current condition of education, if not in complete disarray, is at best not easy to read, and predictions about its future have to be hedged. Realistic prognostications must take into account the many forces—political, economic, and social—that interact constantly to give

1

schools direction, shape, and substance; the full impact of each of these is hard to assess.

Nevertheless, what society expects of its institutions is ultimately what society gets. Currently, American society is uncertain about how good the schools are and confused over what it should expect of them. The one thing that does seem certain, however, is that the American people want more than they have been getting. Consequently, they no longer intend to leave the destiny of public schools in the hands of professional educators. That is one of the messages of the Proposition 13 response. It is even more evident in the headlines and stories that appear in the daily press. Few topics surpass education in extent and diversity of coverage. The people are indeed concerned and speaking out, though with many different voices.

In this volume I have attempted to analyze what these voices are saying and to sort out from all the diverse criticism, activities, movements, and forces focused on public education what its real condition is and where it is likely to be a few years hence. It is an important time in our educational history. It is essential that we understand the critical issues and give conscious direction to what is happening.

By sorting out the major issues education faces today and presenting an objective yet comprehensive overview of what the schools are and are not accomplishing, I hope to clarify some of the current misunderstandings that, if left unchallenged and unexplained, would destroy our present system of public education. It is essential that not only professional educators but citizens and lay leaders understand the problems, issues, accomplishments, and deficiencies of our schools if this system is to be maintained, much less improved.

For most parents there is no practical, affordable alternative to public education. They currently have no choice, furthermore, to which schools their children will be assigned, once they select their place of residence. Even residence provides no certainty, with school busing patterns under constant revision, nor does it guarantee which teachers their children will have. Their chances to influence their children's education are currently restricted to a few contacts they might have with teachers at conference time and following PTA meetings or by exchanging notes or phone calls when specific concerns arise.

For an increasing number of adults without children of school age, the main concern with public education is its cost. They realize that school expenditures represent a sizable portion of the overall cost of government, and they wonder if they are getting their money's worth.

By dealing with the questions and concerns which parents and private citizens have been expressing, I hope to provide needed reassurance that public education is, in part, a victim of a bad press and it is in better shape than the headlines might suggest. Not overlooking its deficiencies and problems, I attempt to build a persuasive case for the directions it must take if it is to attain the full health my earlier predictions suggested. Whether or not full health is achieved depends in great part on the kind of community understanding and support the schools receive.

The book is so laid out that the criticisms and presumed deficiencies are examined first. Chapter 1 presents both the major criticisms of education, as I have heard them, and, after reviewing the most relevant evidence, my judgment about their soundness. In Chapter 2, I explore the reasons why some of the charges are true and why the schools have failed to meet critics' expectations.

Chapter 3 is devoted to reporting what schools do teach with more or less success, what research, meager as it is, seems to indicate about the qualities of good teaching, and what can be done to improve overall school performance. I also attempt to compare the effectiveness of our schools today with those of earlier years and those of other countries.

In the final chapter, I look ahead to where public education is likely to go during the next decade or so. The crystal ball is somewhat fuzzy, I must admit. Some of the uncertainty has to do with how much parents, citizens, and lay leaders will influence the political and professional leadership in one direction or another. The direction of such influence will vary with one's understanding of the major issues surrounding public education and assessment of the validity of the charges which have been leveled at it. My hope in writing this book is to enhance that understanding and improve the assessment.

I wish to express thanks to William Bayles, Theodore Caplow, and Beverly and Kenneth Thompson for their constructive criticisms of early drafts. I appreciate the assistance of colleagues too numerous to mention in tracking down needed information or providing constructive suggestions about particular passages. The manuscript is much improved as a result. Thanks go also to Samuel Crowell, Rebecca Shifflett, and Mary Shelton for their very helpful bibliographic and clerical assistance.

January, 1981   Richard M. Brandt
University of Virginia

Chapter 1

CHARGES AND EVIDENCE

The quality of public-school education in the United States
has been declining for the last decade and a half. This almost
universal decline has been marked by plummeting Scholastic
Aptitude Test scores, functionally illiterate high-school
graduates and the general alienation of many students. It has
been paralleled by an explosive growth in the nonteaching
school bureaucracy, over-all cost increases vastly exceeding
inflation, declining enrollments and a radical redefinition of
school objectives.[1]

Public education is under attack as never before. Scarcely a day
goes by that the local newspaper does not cite someone blaming the
schools for today's high crime rates, widespread illiteracy, and, last but
far from least, rising taxes. Scathing letters to the editor single out lack
of discipline and various "educational innovations"—the current
replacement for open education and, earlier, progressive education—as
the root of all troubles among teenagers and young adults. Popular
periodicals feature in-depth analyses of the demoralized, decadent,
ineffective state of the public schools. Strikes by teachers, as a result of
the bankrupt Chicago schools being unable to meet the 1980 payroll,
highlight the lack of public support on the one hand and question the
professional dedication of educators on the other.

In many older communities, teachers with six-, seven-, and
eight-years seniority have been let go, as declining enrollments force
cutbacks which, in turn, deprive the schools of their most vigorous,
up-to-date, and recently trained talent. Elsewhere, teachers with many
years of successful experience have voluntarily quit their posts and
attempted to start other careers, demoralized over the burdens of
increasing paperwork, directionless administration, unruly and
disinterested youngsters, and mounting public hostility. Despite the
much publicized oversupply of teachers, a national survey in fall, 1977,
identified over nine thousand positions that were unfilled because no
qualified candidates were available. Special education, bilingual
education, and mathematics teachers were in especially short supply.[2]
Increasing shortages in an expanding list of teaching fields are predicted
for the mid-eighties.

If these signs are to be believed, the joy of teaching is apparently
gone. The thrill of learning, if it ever existed except in nostalgic

retrospect, is missing. Schools are out of control. Public education is under indictment for its waste and lack of performance.

Teaching, viewed over the centuries as one of the greatest of callings for intellectually gifted and altruistically oriented adults, now commands relatively low status among white-collar workers. It is increasingly identified with organized labor rather than the professions.

Education, the primary vehicle for social reform during the Kennedy and Lyndon B. Johnson years, is overpowered by society's ills and its obligations to correct them. Instead of educating young people for effective citizenship and productive work-lives, our schools have become the training grounds for crime and anarchy and the breeders of illiteracy and irresponsibility.

What has happened? Are the charges really true; or is the press merely exaggerating the newsworthy, bizarre, and unusual, which results in a false impression of the state of public education? Are the schools bearing the brunt of unwarranted, unjustified criticism? To the extent that the critics are right, where does the blame lie? How much of it is with the professional educator? Who else is responsible? Is there any joy left in teaching, and if not, can it be regained? How can public confidence in the public schools be restored?

The charges and complaints seem too sweeping and extreme to be taken literally and without careful assessment. Our system of public schools is too important to be allowed to disintegrate without an attempt being made to review its strengths as well as its shortcomings and its basic missions along with its other preoccupations, hopefully to piece it back together with its health restored. No alternative institutions are opting for its place; so, if anything constructive is to occur, it will most likely happen within the context of our present system.

My analysis begins with a look at the criticisms and how they are documented. Major charges will be reviewed one at a time. I shall attempt to determine their validity by examining evidence used by the critics and searching for more complete and unbiased information from research. I shall assess the relevance of their evidence within the context of other significant data.

Education is still more art than science, and research answers to educational questions are more imprecise than we would prefer. Many of the answers will depend on which research seems relevant, a matter of professional judgment. If such a process seems too nebulous, one should remember that bringing relevant facts to bear on practical issues is the essence of what all professionals do. Although medicine and law, for example, have solid research foundations, the role of the doctor or lawyer is to select from all the facts available, and from his knowledge of his field, those which are most applicable to a particular situation.

Education, admittedly, may be less advanced in its scientific base than engineering or medicine. It may require less technical knowledge of its practitioners than law, but it certainly is as precise and predictable as economics or long-range weather-forecasting. Just as one can predict that prices will go up when supply dwindles, *if all other relevant variables such as demand remain the same,* one can predict that a pupil will work harder toward solution of a series of problems if he succeeds on one part of it than if he fails, *all other variables being unchanged.*

The "catch," of course, in both of these situations is the italicized clause. Seldom do things remain the same for long. Classrooms are very complex places where many factors interact. Variables are always changing. The nature of the child, the subject, the learning task; the composition of the group; and the personality of the teacher are all factors that affect the learning process and determine what is and is not learned.

If education is failing today, one has to look at the complex interplay of these classroom factors for a means of improving it. What are teachers doing? What are children doing? What is expected of them? What happens at school? While there are no obvious, universal answers to such questions, they are answerable within the context of a particular community, school, or classroom. One ought also to discern some common patterns in the complex interplay of factors in those places where schooling is most successful. Before this is attempted, let me turn to the critics and examine their charges.

Test Scores

First and foremost among the charges is that the schools do not teach. Especially do they not teach the three R's as they once did, nor are pupils as informed about our founding fathers and world affairs as were their parents. Declining test trends provide prima-facie evidence that the schools have failed.

Just how solid is this evidence? How do the test reports add up? What do the test results really indicate? On the surface, it is an open and shut case. In 1979-80 high school seniors taking the Scholastic Aptitude Tests (SAT) averaged 54 points on the verbal and 36 points on the mathematical sections lower than students who took it 17 years earlier. A recent study of the National Center for Education Statistics (NCES) reported almost 5 percent of the 23 million American youths between ages 12 and 17 as illiterate, i.e., 1.4 million youths could not read at the beginning fourth-grade level.[3]

These are impressive statistics and, along with other such reports, they do seem to support a blanket indictment of public education. The indictment comes not just from property owners and taxpayers' groups but from minorities as well. Black leaders are heard to complain that high school graduates cannot get jobs because they do not read well enough to fill out work applications.

While no one would claim 100 percent success or dispute the fact that some youngesters cannot read, write or calculate, a few lonely voices attempt to defend schools' performances and take issue with the general interpretations being made of test results. Former director of the National Institute for Education Harold Hodgkinson, for example, claims the public has been misled by the media drawing national attention to school failures and seldom mentioning the successes.[4] Former Commissioner of Education Harold Howe points out that while some test scores have declined since 1960, others have remained stable, and some have actually improved.[5]

Whom is one to believe? How well founded are the charges? Do youngsters really know less than their counterparts of a generation or two ago; and, if so, how much is the school really to blame? Reaching good and accurate answers to such questions is clearly more complicated than the editorializers suggest.

It is inappropriate, for example, to pass judgment on the basis of the spelling and grammar errors of office secretaries today compared to what our memories tell us high school graduates were like thirty years ago. The groups are simply not comparable. Only half of all 17-year-olds completed high school in the 1940s compared to three-quarters today. A much greater number of mediocre as well as strong students are in college today rather than in the world of work; and, because of expanding work opportunities for women in particular, office secretaries, who tend to be high school rather than college graduates, undoubtedly have less overall academic ability on the average than secretaries a generation earlier.

To pass judgments on today's youth on the basis of facts they do not know, such as the capital of Spain or the identity of Nathan Hale, is equally unfair and invalid. A geometric expansion of knowledge in all areas during the last twenty years not only makes some facts outdated or less important than before; it also increases tremendously the amount of information one cannot possibly know. Even if schools had doubled the amount of information children acquired, the percentage of all that could be known would still have dropped substantially due to the knowledge explosion in recent times.

Facts and knowledge, of course, are not necessarily the same; and to assess the accomplishments of today's schools, one needs to examine test results covering a wide range of information, skills, attitudes, and capacities as well as to recognize that appropriate tests do not even exist for some very important areas of school learning.

Test interpretation is clearly a complex business and requires more expertise than many critics of education possess. To analyze test results and determine whether children are learning less, the same, or more than they were years ago is no simple matter. The test questions have usually changed. Populations taking the tests may be considerably different. These and other technical factors often make direct comparison of one set of results with another very inappropriate.

In several instances recently, experts have been brought together to review important test findings, to synthesize results from a variety of studies, and to seek consensus regarding how best to interpret them. While the experts do not always agree, nor has all the necessary research been done if one is to have definitive answers to the questions raised above, there is agreement on many matters. Major findings and relatively good agreement exist as follows: [6]

1. Both verbal and quantitative scores have declined steadily from the early 1960s through the 1970s for students taking the Scholastic Aptitude Test (SAT). These declines have slowed considerably since 1975, with drops of only 1 or 2 points a year, less than half of earlier rates. Even though the test has been revised several times, an SAT score means the same thing today that it did in 1960. Despite the declines, it predicts college freshman grades, its main function, with about the same degree of accuracy as earlier.

2. With the other major college admissions battery, i.e., the American College Testing Program (ACT), scores have dropped about the same amount over the same time period in three areas (English, mathematics, and social studies) and for the composite, but not in the natural sciences. As with the SAT, the ACT predicts freshman grades as well as ever. One additional finding is most interesting: ACT scores have not changed for those students who completed their freshman year, i.e., college persisters.[7] Apparently, the overall ACT decline was due, in great part, to increasing numbers of low-scoring students taking the test and entering college but then dropping out during the freshman year.

3. Over two-thirds of the decline in SAT scores (and presumably ACT scores as well) during the 1960s can be attributed to changes in the test-taking population. An increasingly diverse group of students began heading for college, including larger numbers of women (who average lower scores in math) and economically disadvantaged students (who average lower scores in all areas). In 1960, over half of those taking the SATs came from the highest 20 percent of national samples

of all eleventh-graders on Project TALENT reading tests, whereas in 1972 only about a third of the SAT takers came from this top range. Very few minority students were taking the SAT in 1960.

During the period of sharpest SAT decline (1970-75) when changes in composition of the test-taking group were relatively small, a special panel of experts chaired by Willard Wirtz credited as likely culprits such factors as (a) less demanding educational standards, (b) changing family patterns, especially those related to staying in touch with school life and reinforcing school expectancies, (c) the distracting influence of television, and (d) deteriorating respect for institutional authority during the Vietnam years. Illustrative of the less demanding educational standards were increased absenteeism, automatic promotion, grade inflation, easier textbooks and curriculum materials, and use of electives rather than required basic courses. With the latter, it was not the fact that courses were elective that seemed to matter, but that they less often demanded thoughtful reading or careful writing.

4.   One must consider other test trends to determine if changes in college admissions scores reflect a genuine deterioration of abilities for all students (not just the college-bound). In Project TALENT, reading comprehension was actually a bit higher in 1970 samples of high school students than in similar samples from the same schools a decade earlier. This lack of decline, and even small advance, takes on added significance when one considers that 87 percent of the age group were staying in school in 1970 compared with 77 percent in 1960.

Scores in the Preliminary Scholastic Aptitude Test (PSAT)/National Merit Qualifying Test remained virtually constant when national samples of eleventh-graders were compared in 1960, 1966, and 1974. The PSAT is composed of SAT test items, but it is administered earlier in high school, typically, to both college- and non-college-bound youths. The lack of a steady, substantial decline until after 1973 provides support for the notion that whatever school factors contributed to the SAT deterioration functioned most during the senior year of high school rather than earlier.

The National Assessment of Educational Progress (NAEP) is intended to provide test results at four-year intervals from national samples of individuals representing various age levels (9, 13, 17, and 26-35) in ten different fields. Unfortunately, this project is of recent origin so its usefulness as a trend indicator is limited to the period after 1970.

Between 1971 and 1974, the NAEP data show a slight improvment among 17-year-olds in basic reading performance and no change in writing mechanics. Overall writing ability dropped, however, and a 2 percent decrease is also reported at each age level in science.[8] By 1977, science achievement scores were still dropping for 17-year-olds, but they had stabilized for 9- and 13-year-olds. Mathematics scores declined for all three age groups.[9]

In contrast to overall reading ability, basic reading consists of such elementary skills as reading road signs, using telephone books and alphabet ordering. It is somewhat ironic that the public is demanding increased accountability standards for schools, but the ones being added, i.e., minimum competency tests which contain such items, do not necessarily relate to abilities that have deteriorated. Probably much more serious are apparent declines in the abilities of children to make inferences about what they read, to write coherent paragraphs, and more generally, to make use of complex thinking.

Other tests showing drops over a ten-year period, consistent with the SAT and ACT (composite) results, were the Iowa Tests of Basic Skills (grades 5-8), Iowa Tests of Educational Development (grades 9-12), the Minnesota Scholastic Aptitude Test (grade 11), and the Comprehensive Tests of Basic Skills (CTBS) in reading and mathematics (above grade 4) and language (above grade 5). [10]

Almost as many findings turn up on the other side of the ledger, however, with improvement or no change indicated. In addition to the science section of ACT, the PSAT, the NAEP (basic reading skills, 1971-74), and Project TALENT results, which have already been discussed, state-wide or national norm scores of second- through fourth- or fifth-graders have either stayed the same or improved on the Iowa Tests of Basic Skills (ITBS) and the CTBS since 1965 in such areas as reading, language, and mathematics.[11] In a recent national norming study of the Gates-MacGinitie Reading Tests 1976-77, children performed better than their 1964 counterparts in the lower grades (especially in the 1st grade) and only slightly worse in the high school years.[12] Continuous improvement has been reported also on the Armed Forces Qualification Test between 1958 and 1972. The latter test covers word knowledge, arithmetic reasoning, spatial perception, and knowledge of tool functions. Results on these latter tests, of course, reflect changes in economic conditions, recruiting policies, pay scales, and the likelihood of war itself.

As mentioned above, scores in the early grades did not typically drop on the ITBS, CTBS, the Gates-MacGinitie and, in most instances, actually improved. More generally, declines in standardized test results, when they have occurred, have tended to be greater for each successive grade after grade four. Possible explanations include (a) greater test coverage of what children are expected to learn at the lower than at the higher grade levels, (b) better teaching in the lower grades, (c) increasing percentages of low-ability youngsters in school and in the same classes as their agemates in the higher grades due to lower school dropout rates and higher promotion rates, and (d) TV programming for young children which is closer to what schools teach than it is for older children.

Some of the apparent discrepancies in test trends from one study to another reflect age differences resulting from changing promotion standards. Early in the century youngsters were older, on the average, in the upper grades than today, because more were retained rather than promoted from one grade to the next. As a result, fourth-grade reading achievement scores in 1957 were below those of two decades earlier, but the scores of 10-year-olds in 1957 were above those of 10-year-olds in 1937. [13] Other discrepancies stem from the populations sampled (college bound, non-college bound, minority groups, etc.). Still others are a function of different abilities and knowledge areas being tapped; some are merely the result of different types of test questions.

The Project TALENT findings deserve a closer look, not merely because they are somewhat reassuring but because attempts were made to correct some of the deficiencies of previous cross-age, cross-generation, comparative research. In this massive study, initiated in the late 1950s, (a) the same students were measured as they progressed through high school and into adult life, and (b) the same tests and questions were used with different generations of students. The first feature was obviously designed to address the complaint cited earlier that samplings of students at different points in time are not really comparable because of changes in the composition of a school as a whole or of those who take the test. The second feature insures not comparing what students know about oranges in one year with what they know about apples in another. In addition to possessing these rather unique features, Project TALENT was quite similar to other national assessment efforts in the types of tests used and the range of abilities tested. Schools were selected to cover the full range of American neighborhoods and communities and, especially, to provide representative samples of regional and socioeconomic patterns.

The 13,000 students who took the test of reading comprehension in 1970, whose scores were weighted to reflect the overall high school population of the country, actually tested slightly higher than their 1960 counterparts. A considerably smaller number, i.e., 1,800 students (grades 9, 10, 11) in 17 schools from the original 1960 samples, also took many of the same tests in 1975, with the following results:

1. Reading comprehension was only a fraction lower in 1975 than in 1960 (half a point in mean scores and 1-2 in percentile scores)

2. Vocabulary, English, Quantitative Reasoning, and Computation were significantly lower (8-17 percentile points)

3. Mathematics, in contrast to Quantative Reasoning and Computation, was slightly higher (2-3 percentile points)

4. Abstract Reasoning and Creativity were substantially higher (8-16 percentile points)

5. Females were higher in Mechanical Reasoning and Visualization (7 and 4 percentile points respectively), and males were slightly lower (2 and 1 points) although still above the females in these qualities.[14]

It is obvious again, from the above results, that student abilities and achievements have not deteriorated "across the board," as the public would seem to believe. Some abilities apparently have dropped somewhat, it is true, but others have improved considerably. The drop in vocabulary suggests less overall reading by students, in and out of school, and the negative influence of competing forces, notably television. John Flanagan, Director of Project TALENT, says that English and computation represent relatively simple types of academic learning which depend on how conscientious students are in studying and doing assignments. The increases in creativity and abstract reasoning are particularly interesting and may indeed reflect some of the problem-solving/project-oriented activities and student-selected curriculum innovations of the last decade. Particularly noteworthy is the fact that the two most important abilities for effectiveness in adult life, reading comprehension and mathematics, have been relatively stable, according to the Project TALENT data.

In a most provocative analysis of test trends, Jencks [15], reaches the conclusion that the SAT decline is relatively unimportant because, as an aptitude test, it measures many things that schools never attempt to teach, such as verbal analogies and puzzle-solving. Citing the National Assessment results and the Iowa state-wide testing program findings for second-, third-, and fourth-graders, he indicates that elementary school children actually made progress in the three R's between 1970 and 1974.

The trouble was at the high school level and in two areas particularly: (a) they were less informed overall, retaining fewer facts about literature, history, contemporary life or scientific subjects, and (b) they were less able to use or respond to complex thought, i.e., make inferences about an author's intent, synthesize a set of diverse ideas, and use reference works. They could punctuate and spell as well, but their writing was less coherent. The solution, argues Jencks, is not in a return to the "basics," which stress repetitive drill on simple words and problems, but to concentrate on more complex skills and ideas. It is the latter that are deteriorating. A "back to the basics" movement could actually accelerate the deterioration by discouraging interest in complex ideas.[16]

Obviously then, to summarize the evidence on the charge that student achievement has fallen drastically over the last couple of decades and the schools are at fault, I must conclude that the charge is highly misleading and vastly overstated. Even in areas where some deterioration seems to have occurred, the evidence is anything but overwhelming, and there are solid reasons other than poor teaching why test scores might have dropped. The test results are clearly not as damning as the critics would make them out. Quite the contrary, they are often reassuring. The unequivocal answer to the CBS news special of August, 1978, "Is anyone out there learning?" is a loud "Yes."

The SAT is not really a good measure for judging how well high schools are doing their job, because it contains many items that schools make no attempt to teach. Conversely, much of what the schools do teach is not covered at all by college admissions tests. The latter are designed solely to predict college grades and, as such, they do a fair job. They are not designed, nor are they the appropriate measure, to assess the effectiveness of our school system.

In many of the "basics" youngsters are doing as well or better than they did in past years. The National Assessment of Educational Progress reports 9-year-olds improving in reading between 1971 and 1975 and relatively unchanged scores for 13- and 17-year-olds.[17] Similar gains are reflected in the results of McGraw-Hill's Comprehensive Test of Basic Skills in second-, third-, and fourth-grade reading and mathematics. The Iowa state-wide testing program, as comprehensive as any, shows continued progress during the primary grades. Even at the secondary level youngsters did better on certain basics in 1974 than in 1971.

My analysis so far has focused only on trends in the 1960s and 1970s, the period of greatest public interest and media-reporting. One test expert, Leo Munday, [18] recently reviewed "then and now" studies going back to the early part of the twentieth century. Although results were not always clearcut and interpretations were complicated by two factors in particular, much different dropout and nonpromotion rates which typically were higher the farther back one goes, achievement gains apparently occurred in the 1940s, 1950s, and early 1960s, followed by the declines in higher grades and certain areas which I have already discussed. These declines were substantial only in the upper grades and probably have stopped at an achievement level equivalent to that of the early 1960s. In the elementary grades, no deterioration took place in the late 1960s, and today's children are at historically high levels. The 5 percent of America's teenagers who cannot read at fourth-grade level today represents a vast improvement over illiteracy figures earlier in this century (45 percent during World War II).[19]

One of the most recent "then and now" studies found 1976 Indiana sixth- and tenth-graders performing as well on the Iowa Silent Reading Tests, at both grade levels, as their 1944 counterparts. Because of greater nonpromotion rates in 1944, the youngsters tested in 1976 were younger, on the average, than the early comparison goups. Thus, it is clear that reading achievement is really greater now than then.[20]

The public has been led to believe that simple changes in test results from one year to the next are all that matter. There is too much faith in what tests can do and too little understanding of the care with which test results must be interpreted.

But with public accountability demands growing, it is very tempting to use standardized tests as the primary means of assessing the products of education. Whether the tests are sufficiently valid for such tasks, especially in the absence of better criteria, is certainly debatable. Teachers, with the most to lose, state a loud "No," pointing to the ambiguity of many questions, their typically middle-class bias, and their unrelatedness to the content of what is being taught. The National Education Association, the National School Boards Association, and many administrators cite the heavy costs in mass testing tens of millions of students annually and take issue with the widespread use of standardized tests to compare the performances of school systems, individual schools and even teachers.[21] The test-publishing industry is estimated to gross 120 million dollars annually for designing, selling, and scoring standardized tests.

In response to increased test criticism and threats to continued market acceptance of standardized tests, the industry is taking steps to improve public understanding of the meaning of test scores and to improve the quality of interpretation of test results. Educational Testing Service (ETS), for example, is developing a new testing and interpretation system to replace the "grade equivalent scores." The latter term has long conveyed misleading information regarding student status. A third-grader who receives a grade equivalent score of 5.2 on a third-grade reading test probably would not score as well on a fifth-grade test. Extrapolations downward are equally erroneous. All one knows is that he did well or poorly on a third-grade test. Under ETS's new system, each child will take a short, 15-item locator test to determine whether the main tests to be taken will be the second-, third-, or fourth-grade tests.

In addition to improvements in standardized tests of the norm-based variety, where items are selected which discriminate among people and spread out a population, competency and criterion-based tests are being developed to permit assessment of whether or not specific objectives are attained. Criterion test items do not necessarily discriminate among people; they only indicate what has to be done to meet minimal performance requirements, e.g., "parallel park a car within a prescribed space in a prescribed time" or "spell 10 words selected at random from a larger list with no more than 2 misspellings."

Many of the state or local school district minimal competency examinations being developed as part of the high school graduation requirements are of the criterion-referenced rather than norm-based variety. It is not certain that this movement to identify and specify what a diploma stands for in minimum competency standards will grow and expand in the years ahead. As with norm-based testing, it has limitations and is sure to add further confusion regarding how well the schools are doing if the public does not understand what competencies are and are not included or if it does not accept the notion of minimum rather than maximum competency assessment.

Tests, whatever their variety, can be useful tools, but there must be realistic expectations with respect to what they can tell us and solid understanding of what their results mean, if they are to perform their intended functions. The responsible leadership of both educator and test publisher will be needed to correct the misunderstandings of the past and demonstrate better test utility in the future.

It is encouraging to see better research and assessment efforts than earlier ones, as exemplified in the project TALENT and NAEP studies. Many fallacious comparisons have been made in the past. It is obvious that test-score comparisons should not be made between schools, districts, teachers, and children without full recognition of the many extenuating factors than can affect results. The American public has an over-simplistic understanding of what tests do and how they do it. The subtleties of sampling differences, socioeconomic changes, characteristics being tested and many other factors that impact on test results must be clearly recognized, if tests are to become the useful and constructive tools we need.

Let me now examine more specific complaints about the schools. These complaints can be grouped loosely under the headings of (a) child deficiencies, (b) teacher inadequacies, (c) inappropriate curriculum, (d) ineffective and unproven programs, (e) weak and costly management, and (f) poor professional preparation of teachers.

Child Learning and Behavior

My analysis of test trends indicates that children have dropped modestly in some specific knowledge/skill areas, such as vocabulary and composition, but that, despite widely published claims, they have lost little or no ground over the previous generation in such important abilities as reading comprehension; they may actually be stronger in the ability to reason abstractly and think creatively. When compared with all youngsters of high school age in 1930, i.e., those out of as well as those in school, today's youth is undoubtedly much better educated and informed. Some of the credit must be given to the schools; television, radio, movies, and family mobility patterns have been influential as well.

Erroneous impressions to the contrary stem, in part, from recalling how smart those high school graduates were early in the century and forgetting that they were the cream of the crop. The composition of today's senior classes is considerably different and encompasses almost the whole spectrum of abilities. A fair comparison would pit only the top 20 percent against those in the whole 1923 senior class. [22]

But other deficiencies than inadequate basic skills are being singled out by today's critics. A lack of discipline and willingness to work head the list. [23] One of our outstanding historians expresses this complaint most succinctly:

> I think what is happening in education is most disturbing. Students really are not required to learn, they are not required to study. There is no discipline. Many are living without rules, without authority, without respect for authority. How are these people ever going to acquire the habits and the knowledge that can run the country, or run the businesses, or produce the works of art? All that means discipline. I don't write without working eight hours a day, sitting up there and working hard. Among many of these students there's no sense of work, no respect for work, no sense of the satisfaction you get out of it.[24]

How the school supposedly contributes to this deficiency is explained as follows: Because of social promotion, one can advance from grade to grade without learning and can complete secondary school not knowing how to read, write or calculate. Grades are inflated over what they formerly were, so an A does not necessarily mean superior work and a C is about as low a grade as one might expect. Thus, we reward students with grades and diplomas they really have not earned. The elective system, furthermore, allows pupils to choose most of what they take, and even within courses there is much student choice with respect to what is to be learned and how assignments are to be done. The rigor and structure of earlier classes have been replaced by a laissez faire, open-ended potpourri of courses and activities, few of which are the same for any two youngsters and none of which makes students struggle very hard or endure very long. Students have become proficient at finding easy courses and conning teachers into keeping assignments light. The tough, demanding teacher can easily be avoided, and many teachers who would like to expect more from their students have to negotiate their assignments within a system that is less demanding and more permissive overall.

What youngsters have really learned, therefore, is that there are ways to get around a system of handed-down obligations and adult expectations rather than facing and coping with them directly. In contrast to their parents, they have been taught to follow their own momentary interests, as a function of many choices being available and the whole system being permissive. In turn, they have become self-centered and existentially oriented, i.e., "What I think is OK, no matter what others think, what has traditionally been thought, or what expert authorities might have to say." In short, they have been taught to question rather than accept authority, to form and express their own opinions, but not necessarily to know how to evaluate their soundness.

As a result, the schools lack discipline and pupils have little incentive to learn. Schools are not even safe places to be in, with thefts, shakedowns, dope-smuggling, and even rapes relatively common events in the larger secondary schools. Lack of respect for both person and property is at least in part the fault of our schools, or so the critics claim.

Different groups of critics focus on different deficiencies, most of which presumably result from the disappearance of rigorous academic demands and behavior expectancies. English professors note the lack of good writing skills in their freshman classes. Foreign language experts highlight the disappearance of Latin, German, and other language courses. Businessmen bemoan the lack of understanding of the free enterprise system, citing Gallup Poll findings that college students think private industry's annual profits average 45 percent rather than the 5-8 percent which they actually are.[25] Women's groups and minorities complain about insufficient recognition and understanding of their dilemmas. Managerial and professional groups are concerned about the disappearance of such middle-class virtues as respect for hard work, neatness and orderliness, respect for property, and consideration of others. Still others charge that middle-class values dominate school curricula and are the primary reason why poverty-level children fail in such large numbers.

The complaints about deficiencies in pupil learning are many and varied and deserve further analysis. First, it must be admitted that some of the charges are obviously valid. Partly as a result of early research in the primary grades which showed that children who were made to repeat grades did no better the next year than equally poor performers who were allowed to go on with their agemates, social promotion became a widely accepted practice in most school systems.[26] In the 1930s, poor performers typically repeated one or more grades and became considerably older and socially out-of-step with their classmates as they progressed through school. When they finally reached junior high school, they were old enough and big enough to drop out of school and find an unskilled job. The labor market can no longer absorb such large numbers of unskilled and relatively uneducated persons, so staying in school has become the the most viable option for this segment of poor school achievers. The high schools of the 1930s did not really have to deal with the poorest third of the population learning-wise, because they dropped out of school and found jobs. Today, the labor force cannot absorb them, and with no other alternative, many of them remain in school.

Schools were never very successful in teaching this segment of the population and they still are not. To the extent that they do not succeed in teaching such youngsters, they serve a "teen-sitting" function, i.e., they keep them off the streets and temporarily off the unemployment rolls. A complication of their staying in school while they are failing to learn is that they frequently disrupt the school lives of those who can learn.

A city high school chemistry teacher and football coach says that as few as 30 serious hallwalkers, i.e., students who move continuously around the halls of a big school rather than attend class, are "enough to disrupt the whole school. These people get much more attention than the straight kids." [27] Another teacher addresses one "turned off kid":

. . . before you reached high school, you decided that most of what school tries to teach isn't worth learning. You tune out and turn off, and the negative vibrations that you send out affect the rest of the class. Multiply yourself by half a dozen, and even a good class can turn sour.[28]

Educators have tried to make school life more bearable for those non-academically oriented pupils, and everyone else as well, by introducing innovative and activity-oriented curricula and by cutting back on the kinds of experiences that build frustration and a sense of failure. One consequence, of course, is that some youngsters who in earlier times would have been school dropouts now remain in school until graduation occurs; they still cannot read or write effectively, nor could their dropout counterparts of three decades ago.

The point I wish to emphasize is that the public schools are not doing any worse than they were, unless it is to condone more school disruption. They still have not succeeded in learning how to teach the low-ability (non-academically oriented) student, and that is a fair criticism that educators should face up to. What the public at large should realize, on the other hand, is that schools have a much tougher job than before, by trying to keep this rather sizable segment of the population rather than dumping youngsters on the streets and making them dependent on the public dole. In comparison, the private schools, whom many critics of public education list as the models of excellence, really have a relatively simple function, namely to prepare students for college. They do not have to face this population at all, and they even have the option to exclude those with higher ability who do not conform behaviorally.

The current public reaction to moving these youngsters through the schools, whether they learn or not, is to demand that minimal competency exams be passed as a prerequisite to high school diplomas. Recent Gallup Polls indicate that a 2-to-1 majority of American adults even favor promoting children from one grade to the next only if they pass examinations.[29] The citizenry is reinforcing the old doctrine that the schools have a screening function to perform, and they want a recognized stamp of approval on those who have gone through school successfully as compared with those who have not.

The charge of grade inflation also holds up under close scrutiny. The proportion of college-bound seniors obtaining A and B grades in high school English courses jumped 25 percent between the mid-sixties and mid-seventies, and other reports show comparable patterns throughout secondary and post-secondary education.

The grade change has occurred, in part, because psychologists endorse the notion that success should be recognized as a means of inducing additional achievement strivings. Earlier psychology emphasized another principle of motivation, namely, the tendency to work hard to avoid failure. While both principles are sound and often work together in the same direction, the low-ability student soon gives up trying to avoid failure, i.e., low grades, because his efforts are typically unsuccessful. Teachers, in turn, have tried to minimize the devastating effects of low grades by adjusting assignments and grading standards so they are realistic and attainable for low- as well as high-ability students.

In adult life, people tend to choose jobs and enter activities in which they can achieve a measure of success. In early schools the options were limited, and if one could not succeed with the prescribed program, one soon gave up trying for other pursuits. The peer world provided one such alternative, and many youngsters found their only successes in the after- and out-of-school activities of adolescence. Today's schools have attempted to broaden the curriculum opportunities to provide for more within-school success over a broader range of abilities.

One of the by-products of this trend has been higher grades and the virtual disappearance of the old middle-class virtue that success comes only from hard work, often on distasteful, meaningless tasks. Today's youths generally, not just those of the lower class, do not buy the old-fashioned notion that work and study must be distasteful and tedious to be worth anything. They have come to question such values and to feel that life should be enjoyable as one goes through it, not just after the attainment of long-pursued goals. To some extent, the schools have contributed to this value change in accepting the psychology of positive reinforcement, higher grades, shorter assignments with more immediate feedback, and a greater spread of curricular options to fit a broad range of interests and abilities.

In the process, grades have tended to lose some of their traditional and singular function of informing parents, college admissions officers, and prospective employers of the quality of one's academic performance. Such persons now know enough not to make judgments on the basis of grade-point average alone but to look also at class rank, the types of courses taken, standardized test results, and other measures of academic potential and achievement.

Regrettably, the charges that pupil misbehavior goes unchecked and schools have become settings for crime and violence are also well-founded, especially in the large urban and suburban secondary schools. The National Institute of Education (NIE) recently completed, in response to a Congressional mandate, an extensive study of the frequency and seriousness of school crime. Questionnaires were sent to more than 4,000 elementary and secondary principals to obtain details about illegal and disruptive incidents in their schools. Visits were made to a nationally representative sample of 642 junior and senior high schools and in-depth studies were conducted in 10 schools with a history of violence but recent improvements.[30]

Among the findings were the following:

1.   Theft is the most widespread offense with an estimated 11 percent of the students and 12 percent of the teachers having something stolen from them monthly. The value of the stolen item is usually under $10.

2.   One-quarter of the nation's schools are vandalized each month at an average cost of $81. Ten percent are burglarized at an average cost of $183. An estimated $200 million is spent yearly for replacement and repair costs resulting from school crime.

3.   Physical assaults occur at the monthly rate of 1.3 percent of high school students and one-half of 1 percent of the secondary teachers. Only 4 percent of the former but almost one-fifth of the latter require medical treatment. Surprisingly perhaps, a higher proportion of teacher attacks occur in junior than senior high schools. Not surprisingly, fewer attacks occur in rural than urban schools.

4.   For teenagers the risk of robbery or assault is greater in than out of schools. Although they spend only a quarter of their waking hours at school, 40 percent of the robberies and 36 percent of the assaults on urban teenagers occur there. The figures are even higher for junior high pupils.

These figures need to be put into perspective. Although they might appear to indict (a) public education for insufficient order and discipline and (b) teenagers for a universal sense of immorality and self-indulgence, no such blanket condemnation is justified. Crime is considered serious in only 8 percent of the nation's schools, and, according to the study, only 10-15 percent of the youngsters account for all the delinquencies. Where school principals are visible in the halls and around the building and where school rules are well known and fairly and consistently applied, the amount of vandalism and delinquency is minimal. Very few schools have to use regular police (1 percent) to help provide law and order. Regular suspension, inschool suspension, and paddling are still widely used as measures of discipline. Over a third of all secondary schools resort to paddling one or more students in a typical month. School crime is probably no worse, overall, than it was a decade ago, although it has leveled off at a considerably higher rate than when mother was a high school student. The sheer bigness of today's schools and resulting anonymity of their students undoubtedly account for much of the increase.

One other characteristic of today's youth deserves mentioning, namely, the pattern of holding a part-time job while continuing one's schooling. Between 1960 and 1975, the percentages of 15- to 19-year olds enrolled in school programs and those participating in the work force both went up in the United States and Canada, whereas in France, Germany, Italy, Japan, and the United Kingdom the latter dropped as the former increased. In 1975, three-fifths of all American boys (ages 15-19) and half the girls were working at least part time, while almost three-quarters were still enrolled in school.[31] Thus, many were doing both, in considerable contrast to the pattern among 1960 American youths as well as those in other countries today.

It is obvious that many high school students find their time and energy divided between homework and after-school work demands. Conducting a survey in several Connecticut schools, one teacher found most of the money being earned was either saved for college or helped to support peer culture participation, i.e., was used for gasoline, exotic clothes, rock concerts, etc. Almost none of it went into the family budget. He blames much of the lack of student learning and need for increased remedial instruction on part-time jobs.

> As physical and mental fatigue creeps in from a steady diet of 12-hour stints of school and work, youthful effervescence gives way to languor. Yawns come earlier in the day and with greater frequency. Attention spans shorten. Youthful dispositions grow less pleasant. Tempers flare. Coping with one's teachers and peers becomes a formidable task. Frequent absence from school becomes a way to catch up on homework or to rest for the afternoon job.[32]

Teacher Inadequacies

I was more than a little upset when one of our finest recent graduates told me that, after two years of apparently successful teaching, he was reentering college to prepare for another profession. It was not the school, the community, his teaching assignments, or the youngsters that bothered him, but the lack of professionalism among the teachers. Talk in the teacher's lounge was about money, out-of-school matters, and the conflict between the administration and the teacher's organization; it was seldom about pupils and almost never about instruction. His opinions of his colleagues, administrators as well as teachers, was that they felt terribly harassed and insecure. Any suggestion was taken as a personal affront.

"Too many are teaching," he had come to believe, "because they can't do anything else. I like to be where I respect the people I'm working with and am stimulated intellectually. If I felt that I was working with professionals, even though the money wasn't great, I'd stay."

I would like to believe this was an isolated situation, that this young man's disenchantments are not widely held and instead, products of his inexperience and youthful idealism. Unfortunately, his attitudes are shared by more and more people both inside and outside the profession.

Despite some improvements in pay and fringe benefits, as compared with the 1950s,[33] teachers currently are leaving the profession in increasing numbers and are far more unhappy with their work and status. A recent NEA survey showed a substantial decline (from 75 percent to 63 percent) over a fifteen-year period in the number of teachers who indicated they would choose a teaching career if they had to do it again. Older teachers, particularly, are leaving the profession. The proportion of teachers with 20 or more years of experience is only half that of 1960.[34] Expanding opportunities in other fields for women and minorities are stimulating considerable career change, even among successful teachers. Local school administrators report loss of some of their best young teachers to real estate, insurance, retail sales and office work—often at twice their teaching salaries.

As a group, teachers are less enthusiastic, if not demoralized, from the mounting public criticism and increasing job complexity. Grievance cases, collective bargaining issues, and teacher strikes tend increasingly to be the subjects of school news rather than instructional programs and educational events. As organized teacher power has become more prominent, public sympathy for the underpaid but dedicated teacher prototype may also be disappearing. As part of the current accountability sentiment, citizens increasingly ask: "If children aren't learning, why shouldn't teachers be credited with some of the blame?"

Physical and emotional fatigue, currently referred to as "teacher burnout," quickly replaces the zest for service when one's efforts are no longer appreciated. Particularly telling are charges that teachers are not able to (a) manage and impose discipline, (b) maintain and enforce standards, (c) model appropriate ideals of manner and action, and (d) are anti-intellectual and, in some instances, illiterate. That teachers do not read, cannot spell or use good grammar, and are the most ignorant of the "educated segment" of our population are all charges to be seen in letters to the editor and heard on the floors of state legislatures. Three or four misspellings and grammatical errors in two illiterate teachers' notes to parents were sufficient recently to spark new legislation requiring teacher competency examinations for the entire Commonwealth of Virginia. When public credibility disappears, it does not take much ammunition to shoot down long-established traditions and stimulate hastily designed, shotgun solutions to public problems.

Another possible contributor to the deteriorating state of teacher morale is the lack of empirical proof that how teachers teach makes much difference in what children learn. For centuries, teachers have been considered as the prime molders of young minds, the most important persons outside the family in influencing what a child was to become. Nostalgically, we all remember favorite teachers who seemed to have made profound and lasting marks.

Mr. Chips may have left a lasting impression on some lads, but his effectiveness in producing substantial and lasting learnings among all of them was still hard to detect, if we are to believe the results of much classroom teaching research. The deficiencies, of course, may be with our measuring sticks and our research techniques. The tests and evaluation technology we are using may not be sufficiently advanced to assess accurately such subtle and complex phenomena as instructional practices and teaching procedures.

I really doubt, however, that assessment deficiencies are the problem; rather the instruction-learning models we have been using are too simple. They do not take into account many other factors that influence learning. My colleague Donald Medley recently reviewed and synthesized 14 major studies of the relationship of classroom practices and pupil achievement. While he reports a number of significant relationships, none of the one-to-one variety accounts for large learning gains. Those gains that seemed attributable to particular styles of teaching were modest in amount, varied with the learning objective and the subject being taught, and occurred only after months, or even years, of implementation. In brief, he found no magic teaching formula that would guarantee easy, quick mastery of learning tasks. What works for some does not work for all; and, furthermore, to have lasting impact, it has to be applied for quite a while. Teachers typically appear to influence children incrementally rather than being able to produce dramatic and lasting changes all at once. [35]

The highly publicized scholarship of Jencks and Coleman also highlights the limitations of school influence in contrast to the enduring and profound thrusts of family and cultural background.[36] While schools have provided opportunities for social mobility of some talented and able lower-class youngsters, their numbers are few when compared to the vast majority whose poverty-level patterns have become even more entrenched and entrapping. It is with these youngsters particularly that the schools have a most difficult task. With children from middle-class homes, the cultural thrust propels them toward success at school, but with those of the lower classes, school and home patterns too often clash; the child who would succeed in school must do so in spite of, rather than because of, what he brings to school. He must learn to live in two cultures, or he must alienate himself from one or the other. For most children, the home/neighborhood influence is pervasive and the school loses. As one downtown principal told me: "We have an influence on our children up to the fifth grade, but then we start losing them to the street."

Fortunately, not all is hopeless, and despite momentum in other directions, school efforts are sometimes dramatically successful for individual children. With patience, understanding, and long implementation of solid programming, we might still turn the tide of ignorance—modestly perhaps and by slow steady increments—into solid achievement for all.

To the charge of teacher illiteracy and dullness, relevant statistics are hard to find. A century ago, school teachers were not only the pillars of their communities, morally and ethically, but they were among the best educated and most intellectual as well. With few alternatives, school teaching was an appropriate role for single women in the middle and even upper classes.

Today, with many more outlets for women and many other fields requiring extensive educational backgrounds, teachers are not nearly so unique in academic background or intellectual orientation. Yet, when one asks whether teachers are as smart as they were a generation ago or how they compare specifically with others in the community, relevant data are hard to find.

Let me summarize what the evidence seems to show with respect to current teacher inadequacies, especially as members of the press, legislatures, and general lay public portray them, by stating the various charges in question form and citing my overall reaction to what has been presented:

Q.: Are teachers less professional and dedicated than formerly?

A.: Somewhat, as evidenced by their increasingly organized-labor posture. A study by the College Enterance Examination Board reports bluntly that teachers "are less dedicated, spend less time in and out of classrooms, are more permissive, give few written or homework assignments and don't enforce high academic standards."[37] I believe, however, that the natural momentum of white-collar culture from which most teachers come will probably limit the spread of unionism, especially as teachers face increasing public rebuff and alienation. A number of state associations have lost, rather than gained, membership during the last few years as they have adopted more and more organized labor tactics. The less apparent dedication, furthermore, is partly a reflection of poor morale over the state of schools and the lack of public confidence rather than less genuine interest in helping children learn.

Q.: What specifically underlies this poor morale, given the fact that salaries and resources are probably no worse than they have always been?

A.: I have already mentioned loss of public confidence. Other factors are (a) increasing student discipline problems and ineffective ways for dealing with them, (b) more involvement with state and federal regulations, (c) the imposition of an increasing array of nonteaching duties, (d) insufficient preparation time for the heavy load they carry, (e) still very limited resources and facilities, and (f) incompetent or non-supportive administrators.[38] Probably the most important factor of all, however, is the frustration of not succeeding at teaching. To the extent that other duties, regulations, and misbehavior complicate the life of a teacher, teaching is bound to be hurt, and the gratification that comes from seeing youngsters learn in response to one's teaching is lessened.

Q.: Is teacher morale really so low?

A.: No question about it. Older teachers are leaving the field in droves whenever reasonable options appear, and younger teachers with less seniority are worried about holding their jobs as enrollments drop. The NEA estimates that during 1975-76, 61,000 teachers received notices that their services would no longer be needed and, in fact, almost one-third were not re-hired. While the number of cuts was not so great these past five years and the overall employment picture has improved considerably, it is still very tight in many places. The number of students seeking admission to teacher education programs has plummeted also. If present trends persist, we may well have a severe teacher shortage again by the mid '80s. Math, science, vocational, and learning disabilities teachers are among the specialists who are already in short supply (1980).

Teachers are also unenthusiastic about teaching because they are unsure of themselves. In part, this uncertainty is from a lack of what Harry Broudy calls "craft consensus."[39] Education lacks not only proven teaching formulas thoroughly established on the basis of research, but also methods and procedures that expert teachers agree are the proper ones to use in given situations. Plumbers, carpenters, and surgeons have learned from their apprenticeships widely accepted ways of threading pipe, nailing joists, and stitching wounds. There is little such consensus in teaching. Instead, rival theorists, innovators, and an increasingly questioning public only add uncertainty and frustration to the conscientious teacher who is sincerely trying to do what is best for children.

Q.: Are teachers less rigorous? Have they eased their standards?

A.: Probably yes—somewhat. Grade distributions have gone up in secondary schools as in colleges. There is little evidence to suggest kids are working harder or learning more, and assignments are probably less arduous or demanding than a generation ago. Composition and writing assignments have been particularly neglected as teachers have had to assume more nonteaching duties. Judging from the number of college freshman composition courses that have been added recently, however, and with ETS adding a writing test to its SAT battery, I predict a renewal of writing emphasis in the high schools. This, in fact, is already happening in a number of places.

Q.: Referring to the discussion of the limited impact of teaching, is there no difference between teachers? Are some not better than others?

A.: Of course there are differences. The really poor teachers never make it into the profession. Among those who have made it, some are better than others. But teaching is a complex art made up of many specific skills: giving directions, explaining the essence of a theory, asking questions, conducting an experiment, managing a group of people, and many others. Most teachers are not equally good in all aspects of teaching, and conversely many teachers are skillful in some ways. So when talking about good teaching, one must consider a number of things, including what kind of teaching is needed for the specific children being taught and what are the specific teaching objectives. This may sound like educational gobbledy-gook, but it really is the best explanation of why teaching research has seldom shown one overall style to be better than another, if the criterion of success is long term achievement.

Q.: Are teachers as smart and informed as formerly?

A.: One can find relatively illiterate, uninformed, and poorly educated teachers here and there. With schools and state education agencies coming under greater public scrutiny then ever before, it does not take many cases to incite legislation to screen out such teachers. While no states required the passing of any standardized tests a few years ago, teacher competency examinations are now already required or under serious consideration in many states.

What is harder to tell is how intelligent and knowledgeable teachers are generally, as compared with those of a generation ago and with members of other professions.

In brief, teacher problems are very real and would appear to be more serious than a few years ago. It behooves us to examine, in later chapters, underlying factors contributing to these problems and to explore ways to alleviate them. This exploration could easily bring forth a reassessment of the roles teachers play and the duties they perform. Surely, changes are needed if the profession is to survive and regain its health and stature.

Curriculum and Textbooks

As indicated earlier, gaps in student information and understanding are often traceable to (a) the knowledge explosion, which makes it increasingly impossible to "cover a subject" within a semester's schedule, and (b) the elective system, in which students' choices cause some subjects to be ignored at the expense of others. Just as most of the scientists of all time are still living, the majority of scholars responsible for discovering and publishing the various bodies of knowledge that make up the world of scholarship are also alive and still working.

High school subjects like American history or English literature are likely to contain very different material today than what was included in the 1930s. Not only does the last half-century of activity need to be accounted for, but some reordering and reselection of previous information are appropriate in keeping with later and, presumably, more advanced scholarship.

Even in my own high school teaching days 30 years ago, I and most of my colleagues were unable to provide adequate coverage of World War I or afterwards because we had spent too much time on the early periods of American History. The point being made is that curriculum content and text materials are, and always were, heavily dependent on the selection of what is to be taught out of a vast domain of possibilities. That domain has increased geometrically in size, depth, and scope, in keeping with the number of scholars at work. Reaching consensus regarding what knowledge youngsters need to acquire has become increasingly difficult.

The prime curriculum complaint being raised at the moment is one typically heard after every period of educational innovation; namely, not enough of the "basics" are being taught. Although critics have voiced this complaint for decades, recent publicity over test trends and taxes has roused school boards to action as never before. With the new math apparently failing to teach boys and girls to calculate (not really its primary objective), open education as deficient in discipline and order as the progressive education of the thirties, and youngsters applying for jobs and even entering college without being able to read, write, spell or use correct grammar, the public outcry is for a return to the "basics."

In state after state and community after community, the public is demanding that competency tests be faced and mastered before diplomas are granted. The problem is not so much with the need for mastery tests as how to choose or develop them. What particular knowledge and skills are sufficiently critical, in comparison to others, to be included in the assessment battery? What performance standards should be established, and who should set them? There is hot debate over these questions. In some localities, mastery assessment focuses on "life" skills such as "swimming 50 yards" and "using a telephone book correctly." In others the concentration is on the academic areas of reading, writing, spelling, calculating, and being informed about historical events, literary figures, and other traditional high school topics.

In all instances, selecting or developing the tests and deciding what should be considered minimal passing scores raise difficult yet critical questions. Does one choose sixth-grade reading level, for example, knowing that this is sufficient to permit a reasonable understanding of most newspapers, popular journals and other consumer literature or does one select ninth-grade or higher levels on the premise that standards should be sufficient to make people struggle and the diploma mean something? Whatever is chosen will be arbitrary, nor will it specify anywhere near a full understanding of what a young person can or cannot know.

Even at the sixth-grade level, some 18-year-olds will fail. Despite the best remedial efforts, some youngsters will fail.[40] Some but not all of those failing would be classified as mentally retarded. Philosophically, are we discriminating against the handicapped if we set barriers to a high school diploma that for some youngsters will indeed be unreachable?

The higher the standards, of course, the more failures. The failing percentages, it should be realized, will be much greater in the mountain communities of Appalachia than the suburbs of Washington, Charleston, or Pittsburgh, if the same standards are used.

Is it fair to children in Wise County, Virginia, in the heart of Appalachia where only 70 percent of the eleventh-grade class score at the ninth-grade level or better compared to 87 percent for Fairfax, Virginia, youngsters?[41] The question of local versus state standards, not to mention the possibility of national ones, is very real and the subject of much current debate.

No matter what level is established, one must realize that a relatively small percentage of youngsters will be challenged to meet it. If it is set well below grade level, most youngsters will pass it with no effort, and their real abilities will not be challenged or identified. Some, as indicated above, will have little chance of passing, even after great struggle, so despair rather than challenge will result. For a minority of the population, i.e., those within reasonable reach of the standard, the tests might serve as a positive and constructive motivator. As Brickell states it:

> A single standard can be too hard for a dull student, yet be too easy for a bright student: impossible for the dull and thus not motivating, trivial for the bright and thus not motivating, be objectionable to parents and teachers of the dull, laughable to parents and teachers of the bright, and thus acceptable to none of them.[42]

The setting of minimal competency standards as requirements for securing diplomas makes the schools once again a screening agency for the work force. The higher the standards the greater the number of youths who will be screened out of either further schooling or the best job opportunities. By demanding such standards, society is giving the schools a responsibility it once assumed. It will be interesting to see which agencies society expects to pick up the burden of employing and training those who are screened out; or if, by default, they will merely be added to the welfare roles.

The "back to the basics" movement is related to mandated competency testing and possesses some of the same ambiguities. What is meant by "basics" varies considerably from one person to the next, although spelling, grammar, reading, and writing are always included. Some would add phonics teaching and Latin, however, while others might stress history, economics, and geography rather than social studies.

What this movement suggests is that too little time is spent on core subjects, the three R's particularly, and much is wasted on peripheral matters. What is core and what is peripheral are items over which parents and teachers might differ significantly. Remembering their own first- and second-grade letter- and word-attack instruction, some parents cite phonics as the core instructional activity for a good reading program. They remain unconvinced when reading specialists tell them that phonics may be either an aid or an unnecessary barrier to learning to read. It represents only one of many reading sub-skills and not an essential one. Learning how to break down a word one does not recognize may be a useful teaching objective, but it is not an indispensable element for beginning reading instruction and may, for some children, actually thwart their progress.

I cite the phonics example to indicate that the "back to the basics" critics often have very specific notions, usually out of their own school experiences, of not only what should be taught but how it can be taught best. They are unwilling to admit that teachers have special expertise. While they may recognize the fact that lawyers and doctors have specialized knowledge necessary to their practice, educational critics, especially of the "back to basics" variety, are prone to think that their own ideas are better than those of the professionally trained and practicing educator. Perhaps it is their 12-20 years in school under a variety of teachers that makes them so sure of themselves. Had they had as many dealings with doctors or lawyers, they might be equally opinionated and critical in these respective fields.

Another perculiarity of such criticism is the tendency to resist educational change and new notions about teaching. In many areas of modern life, we have come to expect change and improvment—in cars, houses, clothing, medicine, etc. One of the dominant features of Western Society is technological improvement and changing patterns of living. But not in education. "The 'little red school house' was good enough for Grandma, and we would do well to get back to it and forget all these new-fangled notions," so the critics maintain. Perhaps schools are a bit like mother's lap, secure and comforting in retrospect. We sentimentally strive to preserve them in the original state, whether or not they continue to serve mankind well.

The best response to the "back to the basics" critics is to assess how much time is actually being spent on various subjects and on particular topics. Surveys of what is taught and how much attention various topics receive should be conducted regularly at the school and district level and summarized by state, region, and nation. Parents and citizens in general have a right to know what children are exposed to at school.

Unfortunately, such surveys are scarce. One 1972 study compared student activities in 20 traditional U.S. schools with those of 20 open U.S. schools and 20 British open schools. Classrooms were matched in the two groups of U.S. classrooms on the basis of students' age (5-8), locale, socioeconomic status, racial and ethnic composition, and public or private school status. Except for the latter factor, British classrooms were selected by the same criteria. Significant differences were found between the three groups primarily in the amount and type of reading instruction. In the traditional U.S. schools, reading in some form was in evidence almost two-thirds of the time (66 percent), compared with 36 percent and 27 percent for the U.S. and British open schools. They stressed spelling, phonics, and grammar significantly more than the open schools, and language-experience reading activities significantly less. The U.S. open classrooms, overall, were more like the British open than the traditional U.S. classrooms. [43]

Not only is the "back to the basics" group interested in reading, writing, and arithmetic skills, but in the content of social studies, literature, and other subjects. Occasionally, they will attack teachers for points of view they presumably have expressed; their targets, most often, are textbooks in use. Under the auspices of the Georgetown University's Ethics and Public Policy Center, for example, three reviewers recently tore a widely used high school civics textbook to pieces for uncritically espousing the cause of big government. [44] Self-appointed citizens' groups are highly active, scrutinizing textbook and school library materials for objectionable passages. In some communities they have even managed to purge from schoolroom shelves such well known books as *The Diary of Anne Frank, Huckleberry Finn,* and *Brave New World.* [45]

Critics attack the schools, furthermore, for both what they include and what they exclude. Two of the more popular complaints are against sex education and family life classes, which are viewed as encroachments on family responsibility. Executives criticize schools for inadequate teaching of the basic principles of economics and the business world. The following statement by the president of the Marriott Corporation appeared in *Forbes* magazine recently:

> Today, nine out of ten high school graduates have never had a course in economics. Only five states require a course on the American free enterprise system in their secondary schools. I can't believe that a course on astronomy beats a course on the economy. Is a study of Napoleon more pertinent than a study of inflation? Are French and Spanish more important than supply and demand? We're long on Quixote . . . but not much on Carnegie. We learn about climate in south America—but not competition in North America. [46]

What the curriculum contains and excludes turns out to be everybody's business. The days when professional educators had the major say are long gone now that public education has come under close scrutiny. Those days are unlikely to return unless educators regain widespread public trust and confidence and the critics' voices are stilled.

Educational Innovations

When the Russians put the first man in space, they also launched a missile at American education. Rightly or wrongly, much of the blame for their winning this initial competition was attributed to too little mathematics and science emphasis in our schools. Shortly thereafter, with help from physicists, biologists, and psychologists in particular, schools all over America introduced "new math" and several revamped science curricula. The new curricula presumably demanded less rote memorization than traditional courses and more fundamental conceptualization of scientific and mathematical principles. Working with number systems other than that with base 10, the one in everyday use, and couching everything in the language of sets became fashionable beginning topics in arithmetic, for example, rather than rehearsing over and over again the addition, subtraction, multiplication and division of whole numbers and fractions. Greater emphasis on the structure of knowledge was to lead eventually to both increased understanding, overall, and relatively easy acquisition of the calculation skills and other mechanical operations which had always been taught.

One of the interesting concomitants of this movement was the effort of parents, i.e., well-educated middle-class parents, to learn the "new math" so they could stay abreast of their youngsters and help them with their homework. Unfortunately, mastery of the new concepts was not easy, and most parents soon gave up trying. Teachers, in turn, stopped giving homework for fear that parents' attempts to help would only confuse pupils; they substituted in-class practice instead.

Within a decade it became apparent that no widespread, sharply increased understanding of mathematics and science had resulted from these efforts, and the mechanical skills, if anything, had actually deteriorated. What is left of the new math and science is hardly recognizable as a discrete entity; it is blended smoothly into the fabric of traditional units and approaches.

Mathematics and science deficiencies represented only one education target for national attention. President Lyndon Johnson, a former school teacher himself, and Congress made education the chief delivery boy for many of their social programs. The Elementary and Secondary Education Act (ESEA) of 1965 was the most sweeping educational legislation ever enacted. Its Title I compensatory education money was to provide children from poverty homes and low socioeconomic environments with the extra educational resources, physical nutrients, and intellectual stimulation needed to close the cultural gap between them and youngsters from white-collar, middle-class neighborhoods. Public schools across the nation with sizable numbers of "disadvantaged children" have received Title I funds year after year, totaling billions of dollars. In 1979, they added up to 3-1/3 billion dollars and accounted for about 3 percent of all expenditures for public elementary and secondary education. No other program comes close to Title I in the amount of federal support given to local school systems. Although considerably more money goes to urban and rural school districts than relatively affluent suburban ones, there are few districts that do not receive some funding from this source.

Along with Title I came pre-school, day care, and Head Start legislation, soon to be followed by Follow Through programs. Early childhood authorities, notably Benjamin Bloom at the University of Chicago, presented a strong case that the older the child when remediation or extra stimulation was started, the less effective it would be. Bloom's thesis argued quite convincingly that two-thirds of one's total intellectual development is completed by age six, the age at which children typically start formal schooling. Early childhood is when children are most malleable.[47]

Other federally instigated thrusts included support for para-professionals as teacher aides, Upward Bound activities to assist minority and other high school youngsters of low income families get ready for college, bilingual education, Indian education, adult education, career education, alcohol and drug abuse education, and a host of other programs designed to meet presumed national needs, promote educational reforms or give extra assistance to disadvantaged groups. Title III (now Title IVc) of the ESEA was intended to stimulate school system R & D. A National Institute of Education (NIE) was established in the image of NIH, only on a woefully meager basis. This major federal agency for conducting and stimulating educational research had a budget of under 100 million dollars in 1980, a mere fraction of NIH's multibillion dollar total.

The enactment of PL 94-142 in 1975 to stimulate full educational programming for handicapped children provided the most sweeping school-related legislation since the intial passage of ESEA a decade earlier. Allocations to date are relatively modest, but the demands on school systems to offer appropriate and highly tailored programs in the least restrictive environment for children with every kind and degree of handicap, no matter what the cost, is limitless in potential funding demands, especially if parents of other children begin demanding equal treatment.

In addition to these and other specifically designed federal thrusts, local educators have developed and tested many new organizational and instructional items of their own, often with extra support from Title III or other outside sources. Especially noteworthy efforts have been made with open education, nongraded education, team teaching, modular scheduling, individually guided instruction, magnet schools, and the use of educational vouchers. While each of these provides a fascinating story of educational change effort, it is sufficient at this point to indicate that, in the minds of at least one critic, they all served to obscure the primary educational issue, namely, the presumed decline of academic achievement, and to lead us away from rather than toward resolution of our major problems. [48]

The principal indictment is that educators have tampered badly with tradition l educational programming by introducing hastily designed gimmicks that have not worked. Educators have been irresponsible in their neglect of traditional values and subject matter.

Their innovations, by and large, have not worked; and, even worse, they have built up false expectations and hopes.[49]

Enough time has probably ellapsed since the start of many of these efforts to examine their history and appraise their success on the basis of available research data. Fortunately, sufficient data have been generated on many of these programs to allow some response to the indictment above. Let me review how well Title I programs seem to be working.

Title I (ESEA) was established by Congress to provide extra funding to school districts in proportion to their numbers of children from low-income families so that low-achieving children could be given compensatory education services. Congress recognized the connection between poverty at home and poor performance in school. Over one-fifth of the country's public elementary children receive either Title I or state-funded compensatory education assistance, and 5 percent of the enrollment in nonpublic schools as well.

Most typically, the compensatory services consist of remedial mathematics or reading instruction in relatively small classes averaging 3 and 5 hours per week respectively. Funds are also used to expand library and other teaching resources, provide medical and dental care, support kindergarten readiness activities, strengthen language arts programs, etc. Nationally, Title I funds pay the salaries of an estimated 8 percent of all elementary school teachers and about half the teacher aides.[50] Overall, since 1965, school districts have been given between one and two billion dollars of federal funds each year to support compensatory education programs. Title I appropriations for the 1980 fiscal year were over 3.3 billion dollars.[51]

So Title I is no small operation. How well does it work? This is not an easy question to answer as there are many matters to consider: on which specific achievements or deficiencies does one focus? What measuring sticks are available? How long does remediation take place before results are likely? What is the nature of the remediation?

What has made it particularly hard to evaluate Title I is the great variation in the way funds are used. School districts can choose within very broad guidelines how they will spend the money, and they have varied greatly in this respect.

Evaluations were aimed first, therefore, at finding out how funds were actually used. One early study reported funds being spent primarily on equipment and materials for schools as a whole rather than for educational services to Title I children. A somewhat later study showed schools in the poorest communities to be spending fewer Title I dollars on instructional help and more on human support services (food, clothing, counseling, medical care, etc.) than wealthier districts. Overall, however, three-fourths of the funds are typically used directly for instruction. [52]

Rossi summarized the major Title I evaluation findings for the 1966-77 period as follows:

> Many local education agencies (LEAs) saw Title I as a supplement to inadequate LEA budgets. Most states failed to implement Title I in full compliance of federal regulations. There was little evidence at the national level that the programs had any positive impact on the eligible and participating children. [53]

The latter point is supported by two major reports, one by Education Testing Service and another by Stanford Research Institute. Looking at the reading scores of 50,000 children in 221 schools, ETS reported no substantial difference between students in and not in compensatory programs. [54] SRI examined 283 state reports of student test scores and found that, although during the school year Title I children gained an average of 0.4 months more per month than disadvantaged students not receiving Title I assistance, considerable erosion of these gains occurred during summer vacations. [55] Overall, the investigators reported that "the state testing data show no evidence of Title I impact." [56]

In a more recent study of selected characteristics of Title I reading and mathematics programs, highly positive achievement gains are reported over a seven-month period:

> For 1st graders—12 months in reading and 11 in math.
> For 3rd graders—8 months in reading and 12 in math. [57]

A relatively small sample (approximately 1,400 compensatory education pupils) maintained their gains over the summer and were found to have made a year's growth in three out of four groups (9/10 of a year in the other) over a 12-month period. [58]

While these gains are impressive, and remarkably high compared to the earlier studies, classrooms were chosen only if both teachers and principals had prior experience with Title I programs, tending to load the dice in favor of obtaining a sample of strong and effective programs rather than those which were truly representative of all Title I remediation nationally.

There were two other important findings: (a) Students in classes with highly individualized instruction did no better than those in other types of classes. (b) First-grade children who stayed in their regular classrooms for the remedial instruction did significantly better than those who were pulled out, although in the third grade children who were pulled out for their instruction did better in mathematics and as well in reading. The former finding is important, given the predominant pattern of pullout instruction for compensatory education.[59]

Preliminary findings of a large, nationally representative, longitudinal study of compensatory education students, i.e., the "Sustaining Effects Study," also indicate above-average gains in reading and mathematics during the school year and no real skill loss or gain during the summer. However, the gap between compensatory education and middle-class youngsters continues to increase from year to year, because the latter also gain during the summer months even though they are not in school. In summary, these more recent studies suggest that the summer drop-off phenomenon for Title I children may be a relative rather than an absolute loss in ability. Thus, Title I would seem to be more effective than earlier studies suggested, although not sufficiently so as to make up for deficiencies in home and neighborhood cultural backgrounds.[60]

The findings from evaluation studies of other federal programs cast similar doubt on their *overall* effectiveness. Positive results are limited primarily to schools and localities where programs have been implemented particularly well.

The lack of widespread documentation that, after at least a decade of trial and billions of dollars in funding, federal efforts to assist local schools have actually been effective has produced considerable debate over their continuance.

Paul Copperman, author of *The Literacy Hoax,* testified before the Senate Education Subcommittee in February, 1979: "Virtually all categorical aid programs either interfere with the effective operation of . . . [the classroom] or attempt to bypass it altogether. These programs are ineffective, tend to weaken the local education effort."[61] He especially identified ESEA Title 1 and bilingual education as ready for elimination.

His reference to bilingual education followed in the wake of a major report by the American Institutes for Research that Spanish-American students who were taught in their native language achieved about the same in mathematics but less in English than their Spanish-American counterparts who remained in regular English-speaking classrooms for all their instruction. Cost of instruction, furthermore, was one-third greater for those educated bilingually. This has been no small federal thrust. A quarter-of-a-million children were being taught academic subjects in both English and their native tongues in 1978. Native tongues included Arabic, Cambodian, French, Chinese, Polish, Hebrew, among others and along with several dozen varieties of American Indian and Eskimo languages.[62] Despite the negative evaluation, federal support for bilingual education programs continues to grow.

Equally strong criticisms have been made of many other federal programs. Once a leader in the movement to desegregate schools, sociologist James Coleman recently told the *Washington Post* that it has produced no dramatic improvements in the education of blacks. Gains among high-achieving blacks have been offset by harmful effects on many others.[63] A Rand Corporation study of 23 Northern and Southern cities that had court-ordered busing indicates, furthermore, that busing for desegregation purposes has caused a significant amount of white exodus to the suburbs during the last decade.[64]

Similar attacks have been made recently on Vocational Education, Head Start, Right-to-Read and many other federal programs. Program proponents, on the other hand, tend to pick the evaluation studies apart and jump on the media for distorting and sensationalizing the findings.

In August, 1978, for example, a news release covering a Rand Corporation study left the impression that the entire ESEA had been evaluated and found to be a 10-billion-dollar failure. The investigation, in fact, had much more limited scope and was designed primarily to learn what factors led to continuation of projects after federal funds were withdrawn.[65] What the investigators found was indeed critical of the typical federal pattern of developing new technologies and providing funding incentives as the major means for bringing about change at the local level. Relatively few programs were successfully implemented and still fewer continued after federal funding was withdrawn. Successful implementation and long-run continuance depended heavily on extensive, effective leadership and training assistance at the local level. Positive and enthusiastic attitudes on the part of principals and teachers were essential, as well as their full involvement in project activities.[66]

Despite the claims and counterclaims, there is pitifully little sound documentation that federal programs are effective in eradicating children's learning deficiencies or in achieving other primary program objectives in a consistent and predictable manner. Federal initiatives to bring about sweeping educational reform have generally proved ineffective in helping local schools overcome those powerful out-of-school forces that tend to retard human learning and development.

Educational Costs

The easy passage of Proposition 13 in California was the most stunning event of the summer, 1978, elections. The overwhelming margin of victory put politicians on notice that a grass-roots tax revolt was underway. Seldom have politicians been seen to reverse positions so sharply as they did when they joined the "cut the budget" movement. Within days, taxpayer organizations in many other states were in contact with Howard Jarvis, Milton Friedman, and other leaders of the Proposition 13 movement to help them design plans to cut taxes and limit governmental expenditures.

It is too soon to tell how lasting and effective this movement will be in the years ahead. A Jarvis-sponsored proposition to cut state income taxes in half failed by almost two to one in the June, 1980, California elections. Despite such setbacks, the tax reduction movement could eventually bring about a solid slowdown in the growth of government relative to private enterprise. One of the principal campaign promises that launched Ronald Reagan into the presidency was just such a slowdown.

On the other hand, the belief that governmental solutions exist for most human problems might ultimately prevail. Politicians stay in office, typically, by voting for programs and services for their constituents. I am skeptical of how long tax reduction will swing more votes than maintaining or expanding governmental services.

In additon, the protectionist interests of all those in public office (about a sixth of the total work force) are bound to limit the amount of cost-cutting to be done. As White House demonstrations signified in the summer of 1979, public servants themselves constitute a strong lobby against elimination of programs that would provide taxpayer relief. After all, no one wants to vote to do away with one's own livelihood, or for politicians who would so vote.

The main reason that property taxes were the first point of attack rather than state sales, federal income, or other major tax sources is their local character. Any mass movement starts with local rallies and people talking face to face about their mutual problems and possible remedies. Property reassessments and real estate taxes in many communities have multiplied several times during the last few years, in keeping with high rises in the cost of housing. Such sharp reassessments are likely to produce strong citizen reactions and organized community protests, as happened recently in Loudon County, Virginia, when taxpayers covered themselves with tea bags and presented a budget-cutting petition containing 2,000 signatures to the county Board of Supervisors.

The fact that property taxes were the initial focus for this movement has direct meaning for public education. School operating costs account for the great majority of local public expenditures, and property taxes have traditionally been the major source of local government finances. Community residents, therefore, are almost forced to peruse school budgets for possible cost savings if they would hope to reduce local tax burdens. Although they may be reluctant to attack teachers' salaries, which typically account for two-thirds of all operating costs, they are very likely to question a superintendent's use of a public vehicle, supervisory travel, new audio-visual equipment, or class field trips as unnecessary frills. New school buildings or physical plant features almost always raise concerns over unnecessary cost, even if the new facilities operate more efficiently than their outmoded replacements and are constructed from the cheapest available materials.

Except perhaps for building costs, the administrative and special resource items mentioned above generally represent a small fraction of the budget. Cost savings directives for these items usually amount to needless "penny pinching" which often impairs the efficiency and effectiveness of the whole system. Compared to modern business and industrial concerns, school systems are far from top-heavy in administrative, supervisory and support personnel. In Virginia, for example, they represent less than 10 percent of the total instructional work force.

In contrast to industry where plant and equipment might account for more than half of the operating costs, school budgets usually show 80-85 percent allocated to salaries and wages overall and 60-65 percent to teachers alone. Thus, education is still primarily a craft enterprise, much more dependent on labor than technology. As such, it is prone to increasing scrutiny and criticism by systems analysts and modern businessmen. One states: "Public Education is a 200-year-old monopoly, and inefficient as a result."[67]

Although teachers have traditionally been considered as only modestly paid for what they do, their salaries have still been a point of complaint. Writing for *Business Week* magazine, Waterbury, Connecticut, Deputy Superintendent of Schools Theodore H. Martland points out that salaries have increased tenfold since 1940 and the cost per teacher has gone up while class sizes have gone down; yet all this, "with no demonstrable improvement in the product." He cites the lack of evidence that smaller classes lead to greater student learning or that advanced courses in education yield better teaching[68] As most school systems reward teachers with salary increments for advanced graduate courses and as small classes mean more teachers, neither of these expenses can be justified on the basis of greater pupil learning. He also questions automatic pay raises for each year of experience, alluding to research that indicates one's best teaching is done between the fifth and tenth year of experience.[69]

Other cost complaints have focused on the subject matter and the worthwhileness of certain school content. One of the Proposition 13 leaders, Paul Gann, was quoted as saying:

> Now, we don't mind if the schools have to cut out such tremendously educational features as "Unwed Mothering." We always thought that was the wrong way to mother anyway. We would also be willing for them to cut out embroidering, crocheting and belly dancing—and some of those very deep things that they have taken up in the last 20 years that have made such a wonderful society, when the crime only increases now at 15 percent a year.[70]

During the late 1970s, programs and teachers were dropped or cut back in Detroit and several other big cities in sports, music, art and even some academic areas. Given the fact that most school expenses are in personnel, it is likely that continued budget-cutting will take this form of eliminating low priority programs and activities.

The primary criticism of the cost of public education is that it has grown too fast and is too expensive overall. It amounted to 86 billion dollars for elementary and secondary schools in 1978-79 and 56 billion for higher education. These figures are respectively five and ten times greater than similar ones in 1960, thus a considerably greater gain than would be accounted for by inflation and population increases alone. Even in constant dollars, i.e., adjusted for inflation, twice as much was being spent on each pupil in the late 1970s as two decades earlier.[71]

While public education is admittedly big business, its support still represents only a modest fraction of total government expenditures. Its costs are smaller than those of health and welfare but larger than those of many other government programs. The proportion of gross national product expended for education (public and private at all levels) was 7.2 percent in 1977, compared with 5.6 percent in 1961 and 2.6 percent in 1941.[72] In 1923, however, and prior to the massive explosion of social legislation during the last half-century, public schools accounted for 18 percent of all government expenditures. By 1957, their support had slipped percentage-wise to only 12 percent. It climbed back to 17 percent by 1976 as the schools became responsible not only for education but for other social functions as well.[73]

The voters for Proposition 13 were seeking a limitation on government growth and function, not on public education per se. Public schools were particularly hard hit because of their heavy dependence on property taxes, but the real complaint was against big government at all levels and its major service programs. The public apparently did not realize that many of the programs they were complaining about were not funded heavily out of local funds.

A CBS News-New York Times poll taken soon after the Proposition 13 vote indicated that almost all of those voting for it favored reducing welfare and believed that welfare costs were a big part of their local community's expenses. In fact, however, only 4 percent of local community budgets in 1977 were designated for welfare programs. The poll indicated that other services which voters were most willing to have cut were relatively low-cost items also, namely park maintenance, library hours, and street repair. The most expensive local government items, fire and police protection and schools, were the services that citizens were least willing to have reduced. It is obvious, therefore, that the voters were objecting most to the high cost of government in general, rather than to the particular local services that would be most affected. [74]

If there is to be a villain behind the rising tax needs, it has to be the federal bureaucracy which accounts for almost two-thirds of all governmental expenditures. Only 8 percent of the financial base for public schools, on the other hand, is federal money. The state contributes 44 percent and local communities, with the most limited tax powers of all, provide 48 percent.[75] Federal spending, overall, now accounts for 21 percent of the total GNP; the total for all government spending is close to 32 percent of GNP. [76] While only one in ten American employees worked for the government (federal, state, and local) in 1950, one in six does now.

Between those directly on government payrolls and those working for businesses which depend heavily on government contracts, there are probably as many people with tax-supported jobs as those whose employment is fully dependent on the world of private enterprise. To the extent that profit-making activities provide the tax base for all other services, private and corporate business represents the "Golden Goose" of our economic system. At some point its direct and indirect tax burden could become too heavy to carry, and the "Goose" would die.

Thus, while it started with local property taxes, the real success of the "taxpayers revolt" will be determined by its impact on state and, particularly, federal budget-cutting and its ultimate effect on the economic system. As education receives relatively little support at the federal level and only a modest amount at the state level, school budget-pruning is unlikely to have much impact on the overall tax bill which the American public receives.

The basic charge, in summary, is that the schools are too costly. Whether or not something is too costly is always a matter of opinion over how much benefit derives from it. Such a judgment can be best made in the chapters ahead after I have examined other factors affecting the educational process and assessed what the schools do accomplish.

What is clear at this point is that the cost of public education has not increased substantially, relative to the cost of other governmental activities. It still represents a modest fraction of the overall tax burden. If pruning is to be done, schools will not be able to cut costs substantially except by eliminating programs or letting student-teacher ratios climb. There is relatively little fat in clerical or administrative personnel, and pitifully small expenditures for teaching equipment and supplies. Of the $1,322 average expenditure for each pupil in Virginia in 1976-77, only $8 were spent on library books, periodicals, audio-visual materials and other such instructional supplies. While the salaries of instructional personnel (principals, supervisors, and teachers) have doubled in the last decade, so has the consumer price index, leaving them with no greater purchasing power than before. Thus, proposals to cut teachers' salaries seem neither justifiable nor realistic.

In addition to general concerns about the overall cost of education, its heavy dependence on property taxes has been a point of major criticism from educators as well as taxpayer groups. Property taxes represent a relatively small source of revenue in comparison with sales and income taxes in particular; they are increasingly inadequate as the primary economic base for our educational system.

Also, communities differ greatly in property valuation and, therefore, in their ability to raise money for the support of schools; thus, equality of educational opportunity may also differ. Some districts have three or four times the tax base of others. They also vary considerably in local tax rates, which reflect, in part, the willingness of citizens to support their schools.

Great differences exist not only in the taxable wealth for supporting schools but in the cost of educating some types of pupils as compared with others. Handicapped and disadvantaged youngsters obviously require more costly programs than other youngsters. Major court decisions, as well as state and federal legislation, in recent years have made equalization of educational opportunity almost the prime objective for school-financing plans.

Arguments abound over which form of equalization is best, who will bear the tax burden, and which types of students will receive the most benefit. Can federal and state revenues be increased without losing the established patterns of local control? Should equalization be restricted to the basic educational program, thus permitting local program enrichment as well? An equitable and adequate system for financing education in the years ahead most certainly tops the priority list of those who would bring about educational change and improvement.

Teacher Preparation

The finger of blame also points at the schools of education and teachers colleges. Burdened with a teacher surplus which makes job seeking of graduates difficult, teacher educators are faulted by students for directing them into programs for which there are no jobs, by teacher organizations for not relating theory to practice or teaching the specific skills and techniques needed to survive, and by the public for allowing illiterate, uninformed, and poorly educated persons to graduate and receive teaching certificates. One other group of critics, namely, arts and sciences faculties, has always questioned the need for professional education courses, claiming that knowledge of the subjects one is to teach is the primary matter to be learned in college and that teacher education courses lack rigor and substance. Rightly or wrongly, education courses on most campuses have an image problem and are often labeled "gut courses." Easy courses and programs, furthermore, tend to attract weak students, which lends credence to the old notion that those who cannot do anything else can always teach.

Although most of the biases cited above have been heard for years, several have led to concrete action during this time when education as a whole has come under close public scrutiny. The numbers of students seeking and gaining admission into teacher education programs have dropped sharply. The numbers of teacher education graduates decreased for five consecutive years after 1972 and by 1977 were about a third lower. One result was the closing or downgrading to departmental status of several schools of education. Nevertheless, more than 1,200 institutions of higher education continue to prepare teachers, many times greater than the numbers of law, medicine, or even engineering schools. About one-fifth of all bachelors degree recipients are offically prepared to teach.

The widely publicized teacher surplus has obviously taken its toll on teacher education enrollments to the point where the oversupply came nowhere near what was predicted, and already there are indications of a potential teacher shortage again a few years hence. An NEA memorandum estimates that, although there were twice as many 1978 graduates seeking teaching positions as there were jobs, if the quality of school programs and services were brought up to NEA recommended minimum standards by reducing over-crowded classes, expanding special education, enlarging school offerings, reducing the numbers of mis-assigned teachers, etc., the supply would meet only one-fourth of the demand. [77] There never was a surplus in some teaching fields, such as mathematics and industrial arts, and in some geographical regions. Many college placement offices continue to place beginning teachers successfully, especially if they are willing to go where the jobs are.

A second set of developments has to do with who controls the education of teachers. Historically, education faculty, deans, and department heads have prescribed the courses and designed the programs that students planning to become teachers must take. In actuality, arts and sciences faculties and administrators have considerable influence, and often a majority vote, on what is included. Those who complain that arts and sciences courses are neglected in teacher education programs apparently do not realize that, in most colleges, half the course work is in general education (humanities, mathematics, science, and social science) and at least a third of the rest is in a major academic area such as English or mathematics. In most secondary teacher education programs, students have room for only five or six education courses, including student teaching. Students in elementary programs typically take a few more education courses, but at least three-fifths of their total undergraduate course work is in the arts and sciences. If there is a weakness, it is not the lack of solid liberal arts grounding but insufficient time to provide all the professional instruction and clinical experience that are needed.

Although the design of college programs rests with the faculty, the state maintains official control of teacher certification. In most states, colleges have their programs reviewed by the State Department of Education in order to have them attain "approved program" status. Graduates of an "approved program" are automatically certified, whereas all other students desiring certification must have their transcripts reviewed course by course. Recognized advantages of "approved program" certification are (a) greater certainty for students that all certification requirements will be met en route to their degrees, (b) stronger and more flexible programs, as advisors presumably know which are the best courses for meeting particular requirements, and (c) less overall work by state department personnel counting miscellaneous course credits.

Legislators sometimes become upset when they learn about this process, claiming that the state department is abdicating its responsibility and merely rubber-stamping what the colleges do. They complain that the colleges lack a necessary, external quality control when they are solely responsible for deciding who will make it through their approved programs and become certified to teach.

Teacher educators respond that they do apply quality controls by screening students carefully and monitoring their progress closely. They used to document their claim by pointing out that SAT scores of seniors majoring in education were higher than those of the general college population, but today education students tend to score below average. [78] Their professors indicate, however, that quite a few who start do not complete their programs, shifting into other degree programs instead, and that still others who complete their education degrees never enter the profession. Student teaching serves a particular screening as well as training function, even though it comes near the end of one's undergraduate program. Although most students survive this experience sufficiently well to graduate, some are not advised or recommended to teach; still others decide, based primarily on this experience, not to seek a teaching position. For these and other reasons, about a quarter of those graduating from teacher education programs do not even look for a teaching position the following year.

The charge of state department rubber-stamping is perhaps best answered by pointing out that college programs attain "approved program" status only after a full report is prepared showing how specific state requirements are to be met and an on-site review has been made of the program in action. The review team usually consists of carefully chosen faculty from other colleges, experienced teachers, administrators, and state department personnel. During the visits, course syllabi, student records, facilities, and training procedures are examined, and critic teachers and students are interviewed. Review teams talk not only with education professors but arts and sciences faculty and university administrators as well, in order to assess the extent of institutional commitment to teacher education. While the turndown rate may not seem particularly high in relation to the oversupply of teachers, it is certainly high enough to negate the charge of rubber-stamping. In 1978-79, for example, 8 percent of the programs reviewed in Virginia failed to receive unconditional approval. In addition, the state department spot checks transcripts to ensure that graduates are indeed following the programs that were approved. Approved programs are monitored, therefore, and are required to be reviewed every few years to retain their status.

One other quality control measure, of course, comes into play during the hiring and placement of graduates. School districts do indeed discriminate between institutions in choosing among the graduates. In contrast to what others may be saying, most school superintendents feel that today's graduates, overall, are better prepared for teaching than ever before.

Teacher organizations represent an increasingly vocal source of complaint regarding the quality of teacher preparation. While their general criticism is that education courses are too theoretical and impractical, in relation to the real problems and conditions teachers face, the most frequently mentioned deficiency is specific, workable advice on how to manage a class in orderly, effective fashion.

Probably the major difference between the experienced and inexperienced teacher is confidence in knowing how to handle a variety of situations that emerge sooner or later in teaching groups of students. Maintaining discipline cannot be taught quickly and easily out of a book. It must be learned the hard way, by direct exposure and successful coping with various situations. Although class management principles can provide assistance in analyzing teaching-learning activities, the major means of gaining such confidence is through successful, usually supervised, experience in handling increasingly complex situations.

Addressing complaints that too many beginning teachers are not adequately prepared to cope effectively with discipline and class-management problems, legislators in several states have proposed plans for extending the preparation period to five years with the extra time being spent gaining direct teaching experience under increasingly less supervision, i.e., a teaching internship. When such legislation was passed in Virginia in 1976, a struggle ensued over who would provide the supervision—college professors, experienced teachers, local school supervisors, or some combination of these. The teacher organizations generally opted for heavy involvement of teachers, and some of the school administrators along with presidents of the four-year colleges wanted public schools to assume complete supervision of the internship; but no group wanted to assume the full responsibility for screening incompetent interns out of the profession. The most widely endorsed plan called for college personnel, along with local school administrators and teachers, to make such decisions. Virginia's five-year program ultimately died when its costs became visible and no constituent group gave it full support. What was left in its place was a new state requirement for additional classroom experience prior to student teaching.[79]

Another show of force by the organized teaching profession focuses on removing the control of teacher licensing, endorsement, and recertification from the hands of state boards of education and giving it to separate commissions that are dominated by classroom teachers. Such legislation has been introduced in dozens of states, and a number of professional standards commissions have been formed with 50 percent or more of the membership being teachers. With only a few exceptions, however, these commissions are only advisory to state boards of education at this time (1980) rather than having full autonomy and control. If such commissions do achieve separate existence on a greater scale, the control of both numbers and qualities of people entering the profession will fall into the hands of teachers. This development will most certainly influence, if not control, the nature of teacher preparation programs, both preservice and inservice.

Recent legislation to establish federally funded teacher centers represents another attempt by organized teacher groups to take over control of staff development and inservice education from colleges and universities, on the one hand, and school administrators and supervisors, on the other. Teacher-center regulations require a separate governing board from the regular school board and special elections to be held to ensure full representation from different segments of the community and the teaching staff. The regulations are considerably more precise with respect to the make-up of the board than they are regarding the substance of what teacher centers should do. At least half the board shall consist of classroom teachers. Colleges may be asked to provide some of the inservice education but only under the specific direction of the board. Major features of the inservice education provided will be (a) teachers sharing their ideas and techniques with each other and (b) their securing specific assistance from outside experts at their request.

The struggle for the control of teacher education could easily be lost by the colleges if the political strength of organized teachers continues to grow. To the extent that college faculties turn their backs on requests for specific inservice assistance or allow traditional arrogance to stand in the way of collaborative arrangements with school districts, the trend toward teacher independence will be enhanced. Teacher educators must become conversant with teacher problems and needs and make sure their expertise is of practical value if they themselves are to survive.

One other movement directed at reforming teacher education, or at least supplementing the screening processes for teachers entering the profession, is the establishment of minimal competency examinations for teachers. In 1978, the U.S. Supreme Court affirmed a Federal District Court decision which upheld South Carolina's use of a standardized test of teachers' (a) general and professional literacy and (b) knowledge of subjects they were planning to teach as legitimate for certifying teachers. This ruling has led to adoption in many states, or proposals for adoption, of teacher competency tests. All over the country, state departments of education are making plans to administer such examinations as an additional requirement for certification beyond completion of approved programs and required course sequences.

While it is clearly recognized that such tests will not necessarily guarantee good teaching, they presumably do indicate that teachers have demonstrated at least minimal performance on tests of general knowledge, grammar, spelling, mathematics, and the subjects which they are certified to teach. The addition of such tests answers the legislative complaint voiced earlier that there is no external, quality-control check on the teacher education institutions. Their students will now not only have to pass muster in their academic courses and student teaching experiences, but they will also have to succeed on a state-administered competency examination.

Summary

In this chapter, I have explored education under attack and the validity of specific criticisms commonly made. Under close examination, many of the charges do not seem warranted, others are only partly supported, and still others are fair and justified complaints that require attention and correction. But before looking at what schools should do to put their house in order, one needs to consider who else is to blame and what other contributors there are to the apparent lack of full development of all children. To the extent that the school is at fault, we need to examine the reasons why, before specifying plans for improvement. To the extent that others are to blame, we need to ask why education has become the scapegoat for so many societal ills.

Chapter 2

WHO IS TO BLAME?

Perhaps the major reason why schools have come under heavy attack in recent years has nothing to do with the job they perform but with the fact that they represent a very visible, large segment of public employees at a time when people are revolting over increasingly heavy tax burdens. The populace has begun to recognize and question the cost of government services in very personal terms. A day in May is singled out as the time when everyone stops working for Uncle Sam, or state and local cousins, and starts working for oneself. That day, many say, should be rolled back to March or even earlier.

With rising inflation, homeowners had their property reassessed at 50 to 100 percent increases over a two- or three-year period in the late seventies. Prior to that, property tax growth had been more modest, less visible and barely above gains in the cost of living. It also became obvious that the public sector was growing faster than the private one, and that public employees often had greater job security and better fringe benefits than those working in private business or industry.

Between 1965 and 1978, the number of people working for the government went up a third to 17.7 million.[1] This number represents one-sixth of the total work force. If one adds to it all who are on welfare, have retired, or are on social security and those who are employed by private industry but whose pay really comes from government contracts, one begins to realize that perhaps half the populace is directly or indirectly supported by tax expenditures.

The principal sources of government revenue, furthermore, are almost exclusively taxes raised from individuals and private or corporate businesses. The importance of the latter to the economic well-being of the nation should not be underestimated.

If half the people are working for or are beneficiaries of tax supported institutions, one can argue that the productivity of the other half is what ultimately determines the nation's economic health and provides its real tax base. Thus, each private sector worker must be sufficiently productive to support not only himself and his dependents but one other person and his dependents.

It is only natural, therefore, that those working in private business particularly and deriving most of their own benefits from what they earn become critical of those working in government, especially if the value of such service seems at all questionable. Widely publicized government waste or mismanagement, such as the inability of Defense Department officials during 1978 to account for $30 billion of supposed foreign arms sales, only provides ammunition for further criticism. [2]   Another disconcerting admission was the Defense Secretary's purported remark that political pressure forced him to keep military bases open that really should have been shut down, at an estimated cost of 1 billion dollars a year. [3]

Unfortunately for public schools, fire-fighting and police-protection services, all heavily dependent on local property taxes, taxpayers do not have an opportunity to vote on the majority of taxes they have to pay. Local bond issues and property taxes are among the few money items on which citizens vote; so, as the economy tightens and taxpayer resentment grows, more and more local tax increases and bond issues are voted down.

Representing one-fourth of all public employees, teachers and other public school personnel have become scapegoats for a much larger percentage of state and federal workers whom the voters cannot really get at. If the system of financing public education is not overhauled to reduce its heavy dependence on property taxes, schools will continue to bear more than their proportional share of taxpayer resentment and remain scapegoats for other government agencies which are less accessible to voter action.

Moving from the genesis of taxpayer feelings about increasing government costs, let me now turn to some of the presumed school failures and examine some of the reasons.

Expanded Mission

Compared with three generations ago and the years of the little red schoolhouse, when character training and the three R's were the main fare, today's educational menu is almost overwhelming in both quantity and diversity. It has grown steadily throughout this century. Shown below are major school program components as they existed in 1940 along with ones that have been added since that time.

Major School Program Components in 1940

Agricultural education
Art
Basic skills (reading, writing, and mathematics)
Citizenship and character development
College preparation
Consumer education
Drama and theatre
Health and physical education (Later separated)
Home economics
Industrial arts and vocational education
Life adjustment education
Music (instrumental and vocal)
Science (biology, chemistry, physics)
Social studies (civics, geography, history)

Additional School Program Components in 1980

Adult education
Alternative education
Beauty care (and other specific job entry training programs)
Bilingual education
Career education
Community education
Crime resistance education
Desegregation
Distributive education
Driver education
Drug abuse
Ecology
Economics education
Family life education
Language arts
Law-related education
Multicultural education
Safety education
Sex and venereal disease education
Science (environmental education)
Smoking education
Social studies (anthropology, economics, psychology, sociology, government)
Special education (emotionally disturbed, mentally retarded, gifted, physically handicapped, deaf, blind, and speech handicapped for all degrees of handicapping conditions from mild to severe and profound)

Neither list is complete, nor are all of the individual programs separate and distinct. Considerable overlap exists, for example, between home economics and family life education. Some of the specific items are components of others, such as sex education and family life education, or drug abuse and health education. To the extent that items do not overlap between the new and the old, schools today are typically expected to teach both. Little has been dropped from their total curriculum and much has been added.

Behind each of these program components is a long history of political and legislative debate justifying its importance and assigning responsibility to the schools. For example, documenting the need for traffic safety education in grades K-9 is the fact that 5,000 children are hurt or killed annually crossing or playing in streets. Underlying driver education is the fact that motor vehicles are the number one killer of American youths aged 15-19.[4]

In addition to their educational offerings, schools operate restaurants which, at an annual cost of $2.7 billion, serve hot and cold luncheons to 25 million children a day and breakfasts or mid-morning snacks of juice, milk, crackers, raisins to several million more.[5] No longer do most youngsters walk or ride their bikes to the neighborhood school, as they did a half-century ago. Over half of them are transported from their front door to school and home again at the end of the day.[6] Of the total number of employees in a typical school system, about a fifth work in these restaurant and transportation operations or maintain the physical plant.

The cost of these operations alone is not our primary concern but their impact on the educational progam and on staff attention and morale. Scheduling club meetings, drama and band practice, not to mention a host of athletic events, around bus schedules and janitors' hours is not the easiest of management tasks.

Other social services that are delivered at school include eye, ear, and dental screening examinations and polio and tuberculosis vaccinations, i.e., activities designed to address community-wide medical needs. Since the mid-thirties when industrialist Charles Mott began providing incentives for keeping schools open for public use during the evening and on the weekend, they have gradually been used more and more as the coordinating and delivery center for all kinds of recreational, educational, medical and social services to the community. A cadre of community educators has been trained and hired specifically to provide such leadership. In recent years, federal and state appropriations have been added to local and private foundation monies to expand this function to serve all ages and a wide assortment of community needs. School administrators have often been sold the virtues of community education on the premise that voters will tend to support school programs if they partake of its services directly, not just through their children's education.

One of the most unappreciated of the functions modern schools perform is baby-sitting. Many parents can hardly wait for school to start every fall or for Johnny to be old enough to attend. When public schools were closed in Pennsylvania recently, day-care centers were flooded and parents had to pay extra unless they elected to stay home from work. A large increase in working mothers and children who live with only one parent generate pressure to lower the school entrance age and add preschool classes. [7]

Not only is the baby-sitting extended downward in age, but even more significant is the pressure to keep adolescents off the streets and out of the ranks of the unemployed. Whereas less than 30 percent of 17-year-olds finished high school two generations ago, more than 75 percent do today, in great part because few unskilled jobs are available and there is little else to do. The schools have been fulfilling a teen-sitting function for a sizable minority of youngsters who have little interest in learning what the schools try to teach but who have little hope of landing a job if they quit.

While schools may be blamed for failing to induce greater learning incentives in these youngsters, they were not any more successful in the old days. Those who did not learn or were not interested merely dropped out of school and joined the unskilled labor force. The need for the latter has dwindled markedly with technological advances; so there are few constructive outlets for teenagers if they are not interested and successful in school. Undoubtedly, some of the expanded high school offerings into such areas as beauty care and shop mechanics represent attempts at challenging this segment of the population. Where youngsters are not challenged, they quickly become a disruptive element in the education of all the rest. It is important for the general public to recognize this increased teen-sitting function, both to understand some of the complexity of the modern high school and to appreciate the fact that society provides few work alternatives for school dropouts today.

One should also appreciate the low cost of "teen-sitting" in the public schools, especially in relation to the likely costs of other institutional solutions which might be proposed. Baby-sitters typically are paid two dollars an hour. Two times seven hours per day times 180 days per year is $2,520. This figure is considerably above the per-pupil cost of most public schools. Put another way, the schools are coping with pupils for less than baby-sitting wages and are taking them off society's hands for the major part of the day. Whatever youngsters learn while in school, therefore, can be perceived as cost-free, a bonus beyond the cost of baby-sitting. Even if schools do not teach them anything, the public is still getting quite a bargain.

Two social disfunctions the schools have been heavily responsible for correcting are (a) desegregating our society and (b) equalizing the educational opportunities between rich and poor, black and white, handicapped and normal. Ever since the historic Supreme Court decision in 1954, which made illegal the South's separate but equal schools for whites and blacks, public officials have been under the gun to achieve integrated schooling. Millions of dollars are being spent annually to shift students between schools within the same districts. The figure was over eight million for Milwaukee alone in 1976-77.[8]

After a quarter of a century of litigation over school desegregation and years of busing children from one neighborhood to another, the jury is still out over the question of how beneficial are the results. Urban schools are typically more segregated than ever. Court-ordered busing has merely stepped up the white flight to the suburbs. Greatly increased percentage-wise during the last fifteen years, minorities now make up more than 90 percent of the school population in Washington, D.C.; 80 percent in Detroit, Atlanta, New Orleans, and San Antonio; and 70 percent in New York, Baltimore, and San Francisco. National opinion polls indicate that a slight majority of blacks as well as a large percentage of whites opposes busing across district lines.[9]

When he was running for the U.S. Senate, Charles Evers stated his position most forcefully:

> Take busing. I led the fight for busing in Mississippi but it isn't working . . . . I wanted it so we could have quality education. But there is no quality education. No way. Eight years ago, we had 400 black principals. Now we have 25. We had 44 black coaches then. Now we have 12.

> Busing is ridiculous. They've bused every black kid out of our neighborhoods 15 and 20 and 30 miles away to predominantly white neighborhoods. The kids are so sleepy they can't be taught. But they didn't bus any of the white kids to the black neighborhoods. They closed down the black schools. We didn't want that. We lost our identity. Come on, now, is that the price we got to pay? To hell with that.[10]

Whether or not black children's achievement levels have been raised as a result of desegration efforts is apparently debatable also, even when analysts are reviewing the same studies. The Chairman of the National Review Panel on School Desegregation Research, Betsy Levin of Duke University, reported studies showing positive effects to outnumber others three to one, whereas sociologist James S. Coleman reviewed the same analysis and "found fewer than half of the 'reliable' studies . . . showed that desegregation has positive effects on achievement." [11]

After reviewing various studies aimed at examining the supposedly detrimental effects of busing, political scientist Gary Orfield concluded that busing for desegregation purposes has had no major negative consequences nor has it been expensive, accounting for only 1 to 2 percent of a school's budget. He claims, furthermore that desegregation has had little impact on the achievement test scores of middle-class whites and that rumors of an increase in violence when desegregation plans are implemented are not true, if one examines the evidence. One survey, for example, indicated almost a thousand school superintendents reporting little evidence of serious violence after schools were desegregated. [12]

As a result of white flights to the suburbs, however, and a massive influx of blacks from the rural South and of Mexicans, Cubans, and others from abroad, the largest urban school systems no longer have the capability to achieve racial balance by themselves. So far, the Supreme Court has protected the right of the suburban middle class to isolate itself from the problems of the inner city and has not permitted federal judges to order busing across local-government jurisdictional lines for desegregation purposes. [13] Undoubtedly, the last chapter has not been written in this great human drama. It is likely that the schools will continue to bear the brunt of social and racial integration efforts because, among other things, the younger generation is presumed to be more malleable than the older one.

Not unrelated though less obvious is the struggle to keep the "great American dream" open to all, with the public schools the major avenues for children of poverty to take for climbing out of their dismal existence and reaching eventual fame and fortune. Historically, public schools have been justified (a) as a way of producing an informed electorate, essential in sustaining a true democracy, and (b) as a way of building an open society in which talent and hard work can overcome ignorance and low status. The obvious successes of this pattern, whether they be top scientists, successful politicians, or famous athletes for whom the school served a Little League function, are what keep the dream viable. The greater, though less obvious, mark of success for the upcoming generation is higher socioeconomic standing than one's forebears. Although the odds seem long for children of poverty, the history of our nation includes a recurring pattern of upward mobility from one generation to the next.

As indicated in the previous chapter, federal education thrusts have yet to show that they can improve these odds. Hot lunches, extra resources for schools with high percentages of poverty children, Head Start, Follow Through and other special programs are clearly aimed at closing the opportunity gap between middle- and working-class children. The former are privileged by background and a consistency between home and school life styles. On the average, middle-class children have a major head start in the race for educational achievement when they enter school and receive more compatible overall support along the way.

One of the most challenging of all recent federal laws is PL 94-142, the Education for All Handicapped Children Act of 1975. Under the mandates of this law, school systems are required to provide an appropriate education, designed around the specially diagnosed needs of each handicapped child, regardless of the nature and extent of the handicap. His program must allow him to be educated to the maximum extent possible in regular classes with non-handicapped children. The public schools will have to provide such an education for deaf and blind children, severely retarded and autistic youngsters, children with severe speech impediments or even those who cannot talk at all because of brain disfunction, those with missing limbs, with lack of tongue or head control, and even those who because of birth or genetic defects cannot even sit up.

Although federal funds of about $165 per child were appropriated during the 1979-80 year and are expected to go up to 40 percent of the average expenditure per pupil by 1982, the law requires school districts to provide the most appropriate programs possible for such children regardless of cost. The relatively low incidence of various kinds of severely/profoundly handicapped children makes the cost of educational delivery several times that for normal children. School responsibility extends downward to age three, and upward to age 21 for the seven to eight million children who are handicapped.

No one wishes to ignore the handicapped, as schools have often done in the past due to not knowing how to cope with their condition. Yet, the task this federal legislation now gives them, i.e., to integrate this segment of the population into society, is considerably greater and more complex than educating a similar percentage of non-handicapped children. Furthermore, it is not unlikely that, in the name of fair play and equal treatment, parents of normal children will eventually demand the same time, attention and expenditure for their own children.

The main point being made is that the public schools have been given, and in some cases have even asked for, a vastly more complex set of functions than they had fifty years ago. Responding to these additonal charges and implementing these new programs have been particularly demanding. The public needs to understand and appreciate the expanded list of expectancies before faulting the schools too much for declining SAT scores. Considering the tasks they have had to assume, one might well be amazed that scores have not dropped even more and that violence and lack of discipline are not more pronounced. To the extent that time spent on expanded mission components detracts from emphasis on the three R's, some loss of basic skills seems a reasonable expectation.

The public schools have a mission today that is many times greater and more complex than at the turn of the century. Beside all the new activities and programs, they now must deal with the children who cannot or do not want to learn, youngsters with such impoverished and undernourished backgrounds that huge deficiencies must be made up before learning is possible, and now mildly and severely handicapped children, some of whom have never been in school before and others of whom have previously been excluded from regular school life by being placed only in special classes and restricted environments. Some critics have charged that the lowering of school standards is in part a result of spending a disproportionate amount of time on the poor performers and the handicapped to the detriment of good learners and the non-handicapped.

Competing Influences

The failure of schools to do their job as well as they might, I have just argued, is due in part to a vastly expanded and somewhat unclear, if not impossible, mission. Before looking closely in the next chapter at where the schools themselves may be at fault and at what they actually do accomplish, let me indicate who else might share the blame by identifying other major forces tending to shape child learning and development. Many forces working against the schools and contributing to children's lack of learning have been well publicized by the media and discussed by other social critics. This section will be relatively brief, therefore, serving primarily as a reminder that many forces outside the school help shape children's development. Where learning deficiencies exist, the school is not the sole or, in many instances, the major agency to blame.

Changes in work and family living patterns certainly have had an impact. Divorce rates (over 1.1 million in 1979, up 58 percent from 1970), one-parent homes (9.2 million in 1977, up 35 percent from 1970), dual employment of parents (more than half of all school-age children have a working mother),[14] and family mobility patterns are considerably higher than formerly, all of which increases the probability that children will be stirred up over home anxieties and will have a less stable, less security-producing climate of support and understanding. The traumas at home, as any teacher knows, are often reflected in excessive daydreaming, inattention to work, emotional outbursts, overanxious test behavior, and other inappropriate responses to school routines and expectancies.

Intelligence has also been found to vary with birth order and family size, and some of the SAT decline during the sixties and seventies has been attributed to increasing family size during the postwar, baby-boom years and a corresponding decrease in the percentage of first-borns in the population. Presumably, later children receive less adult attention than first-borns, other factors being equal. If this theory is valid, SAT scores should rise during the eighties as a function of family-size decrease during the sixties. [15]

Many of the added educational functions of recent years have been assumed by the school because the home seemingly did not provide them. Sex education is one of the more controversial of such matters; much debate has ensued over whether the home, the school, the church, or some other agency can best provide it today. But many other matters which were once considered the responsibility of the home, such as driver education, may well be taught more systematically and effectively at school. Driver education, incidentally, is sufficiently recognized by auto insurance companies to permit a reduction in rates for youngsters completing such programs.

Shifting community patterns have also had an impact. Whereas school-neighborhood relationships were relatively close and informal in the small towns, rural communities, and even suburban/urban areas of yesteryear, such ties are far less close and personal today, despite the community education movement. Where teachers, parents, and children would often bump into each other at the grocery store, in church, and at community events, such informal contacts are now comparatively rare with teachers often living miles from where they teach, families clustered in subdivisions and apartment developments, communities less identifiable, and schools and communities larger and less personal.

Greater mobility of both families and teachers makes it highly unlikely that youngsters will have the same teachers as their older siblings. It was formerly quite common to hear a teacher say: "You're just as restless and pokey, Billie Brandt, in getting started on your lessons as your brother used to be." As a result of these changes, some of the personal touch to school life that once provided consistency and support for a child is now gone and may never return.

Television, obviously, represents a major new influence on the lives of the most recent generation, although those who grew up in the thirties and forties were exposed regularly, through radio and movies, to much of the same fare as TV offers today: comedy shows, mysteries, soap operas, contests, etc.; even to the exact, same content in such instances as the Hardy Boys, Tarzan and innumerable old movies.

Television is certainly the more absorbing medium, at least in comparison to radio, and the average number of hours children of all ages watch it exceeds the amount of time they spend in school. It represents, therefore, real competition for homework and reading time.

Former TV-radio entertainer Clifton Fadiman sees television as the heart of an alternate culture that competes with the classroom for the minds of children. "Children are filled with images and ideas that make it hard for them to accept the idea that reading, writing, and arithmetic are legitimate . . . . There is no way of reconciling the vision of life offered by Shakespeare or Newton with the vision of life offered by the Gong Show." [16]

Some researchers report that it tends also to incite aggressiveness at nursery school, if not elsewhere, with the most aggressive youngsters coming from families that are relatively lax in controlling what is seen on the TV set. Detective shows and comedy games with lots of yelling and screaming are presumably the most stimulating culprits. [17]

Concurrent with the drop in family influence, in shaping the child, is an increase in peer impact. In downtown America especially, the peer world has become the dominant force shaping the development of youths and young adults. While its primary settings are streets and alleys, vacant lots and abandoned tenement houses, school classrooms, corridors, gymnasiums, and play yards serve also as sites for the unfolding dramas of peer life. Under the very nose of teachers and principals, teenagers communicate their directives from one to another, assess and assign individual status and roles, and establish and express feelings of the group toward the larger society of which it is a part. Included in those feelings are attitudes toward school tasks and teachers that determine how seriously youngsters will regard their learning fare.

To survive as a big city school teacher, one must come to understand the youth culture and develop ways to deal with it effectively. Much of it needs merely to be recognized and condoned, some of it must be controlled or stopped, but some of it the skillful teacher can actually use as the substance of teaching. Thus, teachers need to know the meaning of blank stares, back turns, eye rolls, unusual walking styles, and other precise nonverbal signals of youth culture, if they are not to misinterpret pupil behavior and react inappropriately. [18] Dope and switchblade knives, on the other hand, cannot be condoned and must be brought under control. Sound principles of teaching suggest that much of what is taught can emanate from, or be otherwise related to, the real-life problems which city students face. Thus, Langston Hughes may replace Alfred Lord Tennyson in the daily curriculum, and newspaper shopping ads rather than arithmetic textbooks may provide the problems for practice calculations.

My intention in this section is principally to emphasize that schools *alone* cannot be held accountable for what youngsters learn or do not learn. Television, friends, family, and neighbors all contribute directly or indirectly, by conscious design or unconscious default. How Reggie Jackson expresses himself on a TV sports program may stamp in language-usage patterns more firmly than anything the English teacher might do or say. Similarly, a child of the streets who would attempt to use "proper" English with his peers would very likely find the streets an unsafe place to be. "He be good" is the only way to say it correctly, in certain circles.

If one were to follow a twelve-year-old from the time he gets up in the morning to when he goes to bed at night and record the time he is in primary contact with each of the major influences, it might look as follows:

		Family	TV	Peers	School	Self
6:45— 7:45	Getting dressed eating, ready for school	0.5				0.5
7:45— 8:30	Riding school bus			0.75		
8:30—12:00	School classes				3.5	
12:00— 1:00	Lunch & free time			1.00		
1:00— 3:30	School classes				2.5	
3:30— 4:15	Riding school bus			0.75		
4:15— 5:30	Playing scrub baseball			1.25		
5:30— 6:30	Watching TV		1.0			
6:30— 7:00	Dinner	0.5				
7:00— 9:00	Watching TV		2.0			
9:00— 9:30	Doing assignment				0.5	
9:30—10:15	Reading in bed					0.75
Totals (No. of hours)		1.0	3.0	3.75	6.5	1.25

It is evident that even on a school day peer involvement is 58 percent as great as school involvement, even when one counts the lunch hour as the only period at school when primary attention is focused on friends. Considerable peer interaction actually occurs, and is even permissible, in many classes, between classes, and during break times. One might question the coding of riding the school bus as peer involvement, but a close inspection of what goes on during these rides will show that, for the majority of youngsters, this indeed is what occurs. Another interesting feature of the schedule is the small amount of family interaction opportunity, except perhaps during the three hours of TV watching if other members also happen to be present. Even so, the quality as well as amount of family involvement must be considered minimal.

In assessing where the blame lies for the reported drop in scholastic aptitude among several contributing influences, a Gallup Poll of parents with children in school blamed themselves first and teachers last. Among these parents, 65 percent checked "less parent attention, concern and supervision of the child," and only 39 percent indicated the teachers had failed. "Lack of student motivation" was the second most frequently chosen factor, with "too much television viewing" and "society is becoming more permissive" as the third and fourth factors responsible for the drop.[19] These several non-school factors were very similar to the explanations cited by the Wirtz committee.[20]

Financial and Bureaucratic Constraints

Over the past century, the small and personal "one-twelve" room schools, where everybody knew everybody else, have gradually been replaced by elementary schools enrolling more than 600 students and high schools with over 2,000. Albemarle County (including Charlottesville), Virginia, had 9 public high schools in the mid-thirties, most consisting of grades 8-11 tacked on to the elementary grades and averaging less than 150 students. Today, they have 3 high schools with 6,600 students. After Conant's book, *The American High School Today,* which pointed out the inability of such small units to offer comprehensive academic programs, was published in 1959, this county, along with thousands of others across the nation, began phasing out the small community schools in favor of huge consolidated high schools that served thousands of youngsters and entire communities.[21]

Not only were school systems replacing many small schools with fewer but considerably larger ones, during the growth period after World War II, but school districts themselves were consolidating in many states in order to offer more sophisticated, extensive services. During the last half-century, the number of school districts decreased from 128,000 to about 16,000. The size of each new district in numbers of teachers, schools, and children went up correspondingly (averaging 230 children in 1946 and 2,700 in 1977).[22] In addition, a need was created for specially trained administrative, supervisory, and auxiliary staffs to manage and supervise this more complex operation and to provide the non-teaching services which were now needed, i.e., library management, audio visual assistance, psychological assessment, transportation, etc.

The origins of today's school bureaucracy were vested in these consolidations within and between districts. Although many improvements in the quality and breadth of instruction occurred as a result, such as the addition of well-stocked and professionally-staffed school libraries, other changes, in retrospect, may not have been so good and may actually underlie some of the current dissent over public education. One of these was a substantial loss of community loyalty toward local schools. It is much harder for parents and teachers to know each other when the size of the school community covers half a county rather than just the surrounding neighborhood.

A second change was in the quality of youngsters' learning experiences as a function of increased school size. Although the range of curricular and extra-curricular programs and activities expanded considerably, in keeping with the recommendations of Conant and others, the overall quality of student participation probably deteriorated. The expansion was typically greater in size than in programs and activities; and, except as spectators, students were less likely to participate in a wide assortment of activities in the larger schools.

One comparison of student experiences in a large city high school (2,287 students) with those in four small town high schools (83 to 151 students) brought out the fact that, although there were over 20 times as many students in the former, there were only 5 times as many behavior settings in which to participate and only 1.4 times as many varieties of behavior settings. Examples of types of behavior settings were *athletic events, recognition programs,* and *fund drives,* and of specific events or settings were *football practice, awards assembly,* and *junior class bake sale.* The proportion of students participating in such wholesome activities as *district music festivals* and *dramatic, journalistic,* and *student government competitions* was 3 to 20 times as great in the smaller schools.[23]

Although the quality of performance of a football team or glee club is usually less amateurish in large schools and the activities more professionally instructed, the percentages of students being active players or singers are considerably less. To the extent that high school is viewed as a time to explore one's academic, vocational, and avocational potentials by trying oneself out in many types of activities, smaller schools clearly seem to offer better opportunities.

Not only were schools and school districts growing in size and complexity, but state and federal educational establishments as well. For the first hundred years of our country's history, schools were not only controlled by localities but financially supported by them. During the last half of the nineteenth century, state superintendents of public instruction came into being to provide some overall coordination of local efforts and, eventually, to monitor the distribution of state money needed to supplement local property taxes.

Education had a relatively low profile at the federal level until about two decades ago. It was not mentioned in the U.S. Constitution as a federal government responsibility; so management of the schools had traditionally been left to the states and localities. A longstanding notion holds that the strength of a democracy depends on not only a well-educated citizenry but one whose educational programs are not under the direct control of a central government, where people would be potentially vulnerable to manipulation and attitude-shaping. In a dictatorship, the argument goes, young minds can easily be shaped to support and perpetuate its continuance. In our own country, at the moment, the tradition of not developing a national curriculum or prescribing in Washington what should be taught still runs strong, despite a tremendous increase in federal education activity. In authorizing funds for the 1979 fiscal year, Congressional committees in both House and Senate specified that, despite the upsurge of testing activity in public education and the lack of solid research information on how well schools are doing, NIE was not to develop prototype test items or measurement tools for use across the country. Such a practice would be viewed as a major step toward establishing a national curriculum and threatening our longstanding tradition of state responsibility for education.

Despite this particular hesitancy, the role of the federal government in education has expanded tremendously during the last two decades. Whereas the U.S. Office of Education functioned primarily as an information service center for Congress and the public up through the 1950s, it began soon thereafter to assume monitoring and delivery responsibilities for many of the social programs which Congress and the Presidents had launched. Many of the expanded school mission components of recent years originated at the federal level.

Expenditures of the U.S. Office of Education grew from less than half-a-billion dollars in 1960 to more than ten billion in 1979.[24] Once an obscure information agency with very limited functions, it is now a separate department of the federal government (i.e., the Department of Education) with a cabinet-level head. Whether or not President Reagan will honor his campaign promise to dismantle it remains to be seen. The amount of federal money going into education is 9 percent of that of the U.S. Department of Defense, which supports the entire military establishment.[25] One should realize, furthermore, that this rather staggering amount is not supposed to provide the basic support for the operation of public schools.[26] Federal efforts have been directed, instead, at equalizing educational opportunities between middle-class youngsters and those from poor families, and minority groups, migrant children, and most recently the handicapped.

In response to a very inadequate knowledge base for education, federal efforts have also led to the establishment of a network of R&D centers, a National Institute for Education, modeled very inadequately in financial terms after NIH, and competitive research awards to colleges and private firms. Of all the professions, education has the least solid research base; and, despite these beginning federal efforts, only about 1 percent of all educational expenditures is in support of basic or applied research. Even at the Department of Education, most of the money given out is not for research but for financing personnel training needs or stimulating and monitoring programs on behalf of special groups.

Although the federal government supplies only 8 percent of the total spent on public education, virtually all school systems have become dependent on such money in recent years and could not do without it. Few responsible school administrators are going to ignore the opportunities to strengthen their instructional resources by seeking federal funds, which are readily available for the asking under formula grants and become essential in meeting the regulatory requirements of new social legislation. Once new programs are established with the help of federal money, it becomes very difficult to cut them out when the outside financial backing is phased back or withdrawn. Most federal, state, and even private foundation grants are designed to stimulate the development of new programs (e.g., special instruction for gifted children), but not to provide long-term funding for them. Once a program is in place and people have come to expect it, the local community is expected to assume the full burden of support, along with its other regular programs.

Through this "seed" money approach, the federal government is steadily expanding educational programs and school responsibilities and attaining increased influence over local school systems. Whether federal money is given in bloc grants to the states to be distributed within them to various schools in accordance with general guidelines or, in the case of some legislation, directly to local school districts, there are always strings attached in the form of reports to be made and moneys to be accounted for. Increasingly, substantive evaluation efforts must be mounted to assess the effectiveness of programs, in keeping with the general accountability movement.

One irony in this shift of power from the local and state governments to Washington is that the number of federal employees in educational positions has remained relatively stable over the last few years, while the state and local governments have doubled in size. Much of this latter expansion is financed through "seed" money and other federal grants. Approximately one out of every six dollars of federal expenditures now goes to state and local governments. Such outlays increased from under 50 billion in 1975 to 85 billion in the 1979 fiscal year. Another fact shows the same trend: Washington now provides 27 cents of every dollar spent by state and local governments, compared with just 10 cents in 1950. [27]

In spite of the relative expansion of state rather than federal bureaucracies, control remains in the hands of those who provide the money and establish the conditions under which it can be received. A burgeoning expansion of reports and other paperwork emanating from Washington, primarily, even though Sacramento and other state capitals design many of the forms and do much of the actual mailing, becomes the ultimate mechanism of control by harassing, and often overwhelming, the poor school administrator and his staff. More than 3,000 pages of HEW regulations were written between 1969 and 1977, which in the words of former HEW Secretary Califano "spawned millions of pages of prolix and often self-defeating rules and requirements in federal, state and local administrative manuals." [28]

Addressing the volume of regulatory instructions, alone, is a massive task. Reflect a moment on what a school principal has to do to make sure the school lunch directive (Supts. Memorandum No. 18) on the following page, is properly followed. Someone has to know what a full Type A lunch consists of and have it prepared. Someone must keep track of every student who is offered lunch and record whether he is (a) in grade six and above, (b) a needy (reduced price) or non-needy (full-price) student, (c) takes three or more of the five food items, (d) is charged a la carte prices because of taking less than three items, and (e) which charges are to be reimbursed.

In the course of a year, hundreds of administrative, informational, and regulatory memoranda of this sort are mailed to school administrators across the State, even though Superintendent Campbell managed, through careful pruning efforts, to cut the volume in half during his term of office. A typical day's set of memoranda covers such topics as school bus standards, count of children receiving special education, six-year special education plan and FY 79 fund request, appointment of school board members, teacher contracts, appropriation data, dismissal of school personnel, summer camps, Virginia school law supplements, summary of bills and resolutions in the legislature, and indirect cost instructions. Some of these

TO: Division Superintendents

FROM: W. E. Campbell, Superintendent of Public Instruction
            W. H. Cochran, Deputy Superintendent of Public Instruction

SUBJ: Change in Lunch Requirement for Junior High and Middle Schools

Public Law 94-105 enacted by Congress provided that students in senior high schools not be required to accept offered foods which they did not intend to consume. The National School Lunch Program regulations were amended to implement this provision in September, 1976.

The amended regulations required that students in senior high schools be offered all five food items comprising the full Type A lunch, but they have the option of choosing as few as three of these food items. This provision has come to be known as the "offered vs. served" provision. If the nonneedy student chooses less than the complete Type A lunch, the student is still expected to pay the established price of the lunch. Under this provision, the amount of reimbursement made to a school was not affected.

Effective July 1, 1978 federal regulations resulting from P. L. 95-166 extends this provision to junior high and middle schools <u>when approved by the local school division</u>. The requirements for the senior high school are applicable to the junior high and middle school. They are:

1. The complete Type A lunch must be offered to students.

2. Students must take at least 3 of the five food items for the lunch to be reimbursed under the National School Lunch Program.

3. There must be no reduction in the price paid by full-price and reduced-price students.

4. Students taking fewer than three items must be charged a la carte prices and those items are not reimbursable. In schools participating in the Special Milk Program, a la carte milk is reimbursable under that program.

Junior high and middle schools are those identified as such and containing any combination of grade six and up. As some elementary schools may house students in grade six and up the school division may approve the students in those grades for the "offered vs. served" option as their grade counterparts in junior high and middle schools. This provision is not available to students below the sixth grade.

The "offer vs. served" provision in junior high and middle schools (grades 6 up to senior high school) must be approved by the local school division.

The Assistant State Supervisors, School Food Service will be discussing this provision with you during the summer months. For further information, please contact John F. Miller, State Supervisor, School Food Service, P. O. Box 6Q, Richmond, Virginia 23216

Regulatory Authority: P.L. 95-166.

memoranda solicit information and others present it, but the total effect of these communications reflects the heavily bureaucratic nature of our educational system and the increasingly centralized control in Richmond and, more especially, Washington. The reference to a law enacted by Congress and subsequent federal regulations, in Memorandum 18, is far more typical than formerly and, in fact, characterizes many of the memoranda coming from the office of the Superintendent of Public Instruction.

One consequence of this shift of control from local to state and federal authorities is the loss of autonomy at the local school level. Although the "feds" have not yet established guidelines for what is to be taught or how it is best done, they have usurped the time and attention of school management, and often of classroom teachers as well, by the many other demands they have made.

School administrators at the district and building level no longer have the freedom they once had to run things as they saw fit. Using the rod and spanking a child, once the symbol if not the essence of school discipline, is now taboo in many localities, if not outright illegal. (I would not argue for its return.) No longer can a school principal search a pupil's locker to look for liquor or marijuana without following previously announced, carefully prescribed procedures. He usually needs parental and/or child approval before youngsters can go on a field trip, be given attitude or personality inventories and sometimes even IQ tests. Under the Buckley Amendment, parents and children have a right to review their cumulative records and have them purged if they think inappropriate material is included. Parents of handicapped students have a right to review and approve individualized instructional plans for their children at least annually. Increasingly, due process procedures must be followed in connection with teachers, children, and parents. School administrators are responsible, as they have always been, for money and equipment being protected and accounted for, though today it is more cumbersome. All in all, both management and teaching personnel are harassed by the increasing volume of regulations they must follow and reports they must file.

An assistant superintendent of a large school system told me recently that he would like to be out of educational administration and into a university teaching position, but he could not afford it. He feels that the only place there is still any "action in education, that is, where what you do makes a difference," is in the classroom. Because of heavy involvement in regulatory activity, he could not identify a thing he had done recently for which he had been given primary responsibility and could claim credit for having made a real school improvement. He also indicated that principals are so involved in administrative red tape and bureaucratic activity, they almost never get into the classroom to see, much less affect, what is going on instructionally.

A staff member of the State Department of Education reiterated similar disenchantment with his role and its importance in the educative process, indicating that the public complaints about education and lack of respect for educators were demoralizing. If it were not so late in life, he too would probably seek another career.

These two gentlemen are not isolated examples of disillusioned, demoralized professionals; rather as society imposes increasing bureaucratic constraints on the profession, especially without acknowledging its virtues, even the leadership has become frustrated and disenchanted.

Education is approaching that state when much of the joy of teaching young people is gone. Much of the fault can be traced to work fragmentation and bureaucratic entanglements; these, in turn, keep teachers and, particularly, school administrators from attaining the kind of satisfaction and sense of accomplishement they once knew.

As mentioned earlier, summer 1978 will long be remembered as the beginning of the tax revolt. The 2-to-1 vote for Proposition 13 so shocked the politicians that they could not get on board the tax-limitation and public-expenditure-saving train fast enough. California was not the only place where that train stopped. In Ohio, voters rejected over 100 of the 198 school tax and bond issues before them, even under the threat in a number of places that, as a consequence, schools might not be able to open. Governors in several states put freezes on hiring and restrictions on travel of state employees. A proposed gasoline tax increase from 7 to 10 cents per gallon was voted down in Missouri by an overwhelming margin. Anti-tax organizations sprang up all over the country, and serious considerations were given in most states to some form of tax and spending limitation. One of the most significant events was the passing of resolutions in 24 state legislatures by June, 1978, calling for a constitutional amendment that would prohibit the federal government from deficit-spending.

Congress reacted by passing a bill that cut corporation and individual income-tax rates, especially for middle-income individuals, and giving careful consideration to the Kemp-Roth plan to cut individual income taxes 30 percent over a three-year period. With support of the White House, Senator Muskie, then Chariman of the

Senate Budget Committee, pushed hard for Sunset legislation that would require all federal spending programs to be closed down within ten years unless Congress, after reviewing them, specifically voted to extend them.

An NBC News poll taken on June 12 and 13, 1978, revealed that the American people were upset by taxes almost as much as with inflation and the cost of living. Of the six kinds of taxes asked about, federal taxes were complained about most, with 75 percent indicating they were too high and only one out of five saying that we get our money's worth out of the federal government. About half of the 1,600 persons interviewed said that taxes could probably be cut by one-third, without hurting services, and two-thirds favored a Constitutional amendment setting limits on the amount of taxes the government could collect. Despite widespread support of Proposition 13, they expressed appreciation for local services and relatively little desire to cut local taxes.[29]

To what extent these attitudes will endure long enough to bring about real changes in the tax structure and a reduction of government services remains to be seen. It is obvious that expenditures will receive close public scrutiny in the years ahead, and various proposals for new tax patterns will be offered.

According to one study of tax patterns in 15 Western nations, Americans pay relatively high property and low sales taxes. The United States ranks next to Japan in having the lowest overall tax burden in relation to total national output (30 percent). The industrialized European nations pay taxes in the average amount of 42 percent of their total national output. The United States ranks fourth among nine Western nations in the percentage of GNP spent on public elementary and secondary education. [30] Apparently the U.S. Tax burden is mild, when compared with that of other industrialized nations; and the cost complaints may be directed more at other governmental programs, both educational and noneducational, than at local public schools, if the NBC polls are to be believed.

One might well question the extent to which changes have occurred in the overall cost of education, relative to gross national product, during the last half-century. During the 1930s, it ranged between 3 and 4 percent. It dropped modestly during the war but returned to the 3-4 percent range soon thereafter until the mid-fifties. It reached 5 percent by 1959, 6 percent by 1963, 7 percent by 1967 and 8 percent by 1975. The total figure was slightly over 120 billion in 1975. Operating expenditures per child doubled about every decade since 1939.[31]

The average operating expenditure per child in public elementary and secondary schools was only $1,699 in 1976-77, even with capital outlay and debt interest included.[32] Critics often blame fancy buildings for heavy educational expenses; yet, capital outlays for elementary and secondary schools, even during the big building period, represented only a sixth of the total budget and, today, they account for less than 10 percent. Although the costs of educating a child in public elementary or secondary school doubled each decade after 1939, generally in line with the cost of living, overall expenditures for education almost tripled as increasing numbers of children stayed through high school. [33]

The major increases in total education expenditures are best explained by the expansion of the populations served. Higher education accounts for a good part of the cost increase, as over half of the 20 billion dollar federal contribution in 1976 was for grants and loans to colleges and college students. [34] The college population had exploded, with more than four times as many young people in higher education institutions in 1975 than in 1950. [35] Other population expansions came from extending the school years downward, in many systems, to include kindergarten and even nursery classes, and upward, in Maryland, Virginia and several other states, to add a twelfth grade. Another major expansion was the result of students staying in school long enough to complete high school. Only 30 percent of the fifth-grade class in 1924-25 were graduated from high school in 1932. The high school graduates in 1975, on the other hand, represented approximately three-fourths of the fifth-grade class of seven years earlier.[36] Although changes in social promotion policies explain some of these differences, the holding power of the school is certainly greater than it once was, with the median years of school completed having risen a grade per decade since 1930. Over 93 percent of persons 14-17 years of age were in high school in the fall of 1975, compared with 86 percent in 1959-60, 77 percent in 1949-50, and only 51 percent in 1928-30.[37]

Americans stay in school longer and in larger numbers by far than citizens of any other country. While some nations may provide as much publicly supported education for a small, intellectually elite group, none come close to us in making education as available to such a high percentage of its citizenry. The tax revolt and presumed over-education of many college students for the jobs they can secure may ultimately bring about some withdrawal from this heavy commitment to education.

One thing is certain, namely, that with the cost of public elementary and secondary schools modest and not rising particularly fast in relation to the growth of the economy, it is going to be difficult to trim it substantially without doing damage to the quality of programs. The major cost factor in operating budgets is teachers' salaries. As elementary enrollments have shrunk somewhat from their peak years and secondary enrollments are now also dwindling, the ratio of pupils to teachers has dropped a bit (from 22 in 1970 to 20 in 1977), [38] and there might seem to be room for lopping off teachers. To do so, however, some cutback would have to occur also in what is offered, because those figures include all kinds of teachers in all kinds of specialties. Only eight students in a particular high school may need or want second-year German, for example, and at some point a decision would have to be made that such a class is too small to be affordable. As enrollments drop, there will probably be some increase in costs per pupil, unless we are also willing to drop the number of subjects taught.

Some communities have attempted to reduce non-teaching administrative and supervisory staff as a penny-pinching move. The actual number of these positions that can be eliminated without jeopardizing programs is also small, however, because they are filled by the persons most responsible for making the reports and seeing that the regulations are followed which stem from the recent barrage of educational and social legislation. Compared to private industry, the 300,000 superintendents, principals, supervisors, and other non-teaching staff, less than 10 percent of the total professional personnel, represent a very frugal management commitment for such a large and complex business.

With education being the primary occupation for nearly 3 out of 10 persons (teachers and students together), [39] yet only accounting for about 8 percent of the GNP, how frugal can one be? School systems, in brief, operate very inexpensively and are not likely to waste exhorbitant amounts of tax dollars.

Arguments might well be made, of course, that the heavy increases in federal contributions could be clipped somewhat, especially if some of the expanded mission programs coming from Washington were dropped. Probably the main reason for most of these programs, however, is to equalize educational opportunities for the poor, the handicapped, and those whose backgrounds tend to limit their capacity to participate effectively in the school program without extra assistance.

Variation among school districts in the value of property which serves as the basis for tax revenue is considerable, and state and federal monies are typically distributed in such a manner as to decrease the differences and inequalities. In New York state, for example, state aid per pupil was almost twice as great in those districts with the least property value per pupil. Even with this extra assistance, however, the wealthiest districts were able to spend 50 percent more per pupil. In Virginia, similar differences exist, with only one-third of the budget of some wealthy Northern Virginia school divisions coming from state money compared to almost two-thirds for some Southside rural divisions.[40]

It is almost certain that the tax revolution will bring about changes in the ways schools are supported. Steadily through the years, the localities have decreased their percentage of support from 83 percent in 1929-30 to 68 percent in 1939-40 and now to 48 percent, with states increasing theirs at the same time from 17 to 30 to 44 percent, and the federal government from less than one-half a percent to 2, and now 8 percent. [41]

It is clearly long past the time when property taxes should carry such a heavy part of the total burden. With the federal government having the biggest taxing potential but at the same time, because of historical and constitutional restrictions, having limited responsibility for education, it will take considerable imagination and political leadership to improve the financial support of education without having communities lose control of their schools to state boards of education and state legislatures, if not to Congress and the Washington bureaucracy. Such improvments in the financing of American education must occur, also, at a time when the public is screaming for frugality in government spending.

Obviously, if schools are to thrive, they may have to do so at the expense of other kinds of government spending. For this to happen, the public-at-large has to feel that education is more important than welfare perhaps, health, social security, or foreign aid. If the public is to be convinced that the schools should be ranked so high, our mission needs to be defined better than at present and in line with what we can do best. It is to these matters that I now turn.

Chapter 3

WHAT SCHOOLS TEACH

It is time to look at what schools do teach and how successful they are. Criticisms and doubts about the effectiveness of education, a sparsity of evidence that federally sponsored innovations are working, and widespread concern that schools have too much to do today to do anything well—all suggest a need to examine the ways in which schools make a lasting impact on their charges and to reconsider what is reasonable to expect them to teach.

If influences from the home, peer group and media are rather overpowering, how much difference can schools be expected to make? What instructional approaches are best? What qualities of school life count most? Are we teaching what matters? Just how good are our schools compared to those of other times or in other lands?

Recommendations for educational improvement should be postponed until such questions have been fully explored and answered with the best evidence available. In this chapter, therefore, I will (a) describe what seem to be the enduring effects of school attendance, i.e., the principal matters learned at school, (b) present evidence regarding what features of school life count the most, and (c) provide an assessment of how well our American public schools compare with those of other cultures.

Societal Norms

First and foremost, the school is a social institution. As such, it has its own organizational patterns and traditions. These patterns and traditions reflect in part those of the community in which the school is found, although it is also reasonable to assume that the school helps shape this larger society as well. The school is a creature of the state, and its governance derives directly from the same political forces that give direction to the state and locality. It tends to take on the norms of the larger community as they are expressed in school board policies, media coverage, parent and citizen response and complaint.

Through the first half of this century, middle-class norms dominated school life, indicative of a solid, white-collar community leadership and a middle-class upbringing for most of the teachers. Educated young women, for that matter, had few other career outlets.

The items that made up the Boy Scout code were predominant at school also. Care and respect for property, hard work and individual achievement, postponement of immediate satisfaction for long-term and worthwhile goals, honesty and virtue, orderliness and tidiness, and education and learning were all well established norms to be taught and learned. One did not have to like what was taught but to study hard and show that it was learned.

This industrious, nose-to-the-grindstone approach to life is often referred to as the protestant ethic. It was a principal feature not only of school life early in this century but of business, industry, religion and even recreation. It was the formula for success in all walks of life, i.e., to work hard, to strive, to achieve, and to refrain from momentary pleasures in order to pursue more important matters. It gave promise, quite often a false one, to those at the bottom of the social ladder. It provided the means for immigrants from abroad, or at least their children, to become absorbed into the full stream of American society, thus to reinforce the widespread notion of America as a great melting pot where people from all cultures were put into the same stew to create a magnificent conglomerate. The yeast for that conglomerate was the protestant ethic.

The school played a critical role in this process. Not only did it teach the protestant ethic and other core values; it also provided a necessary transition between home and office or factory. As Dreeben points out, conduct in the family and conduct on the job were governed by somewhat contrasting principles. Obtaining help from someone more knowledgeable and capable than oneself is condoned and even customary at home, but unless special permission is given to do it at school, it might well be considered cheating. Test-taking in particular and much schoolwork are expected to be done without assistance, making it essential for children to distinguish clearly between situations in which one is permitted or expected to cooperate and those in which getting or giving help is considered inappropriate, if not outright dishonest.[1] In contrast to the family, the school is especially suited to teach independence of action—an essential ingredient in the world of work—as well as judgment about how and when to blend it with appropriate cooperative behaviors.

The school not only teaches children to strive hard and to achieve, but, when they are not successful, to accept, or at least tolerate, failure. The whole pattern of making assignments, having children perform, and evaluating their performance adds a success/failure dimension to school life. The field against which one's performances are judged is typically a competitive one, consisting of agemates with relatively similar backgrounds. In contrast to that which the family provides, the field is relatively narrow and competitive. Most children do not succeed or fail consistently. Rather they experience success when their abilities are above class norms and failure when they are not. By the emphasis they place on grades and other symbols of accomplishment, teachers can heighten or diminish the sense of success or failure with which children must live. The school serves as a major training ground for leaning how to handle failure and success and for making choices which are appropriate for and consistent with one's knowledge and ability. Accurate self-assessment is essential for good career decisions, and school life, far more than family life, is set up to provide the wide variety of performance comparisons to bring it about. More will be said about self-concept development in the next section.

Not all of the school's achievement-teaching is with academics, but with sports, dramatics, art, and music as well. The achievement motive permeates the curriculum wherever contests are held and awards, grades, or other forms of individual recognition given. Athletic and extracurricular activities need not be justified on the basis of their contributions to intellectual development, such as happens when youngsters strive to do well academically in order to stay eligible for the team. They are important subjects in their own right, if teaching youngsters to excel is a school objective. Without such activities, a sizable proportion of the school population would have little opportunity to realize success and to know what it means to work hard for something and achieve it.

One additional way in which athletics and such activities as dramatics and glee club make important long-term contributions to youngsters' development is by teaching teamwork as a part of group effort. Athletic events are not so much personal contests between individuals as they are group struggles, with victories not necessarily going to teams with the most stars as to those with the best combination of ability and teamwork. As in industrial society today, where the ultimate contests are between the teams that put together Ford Pintos and GM Chevettes, first-place athletic winners are generally teams, not individuals. Bowl games are typically better-played and more interesting to watch than all-star games. Although the latter display more individual talent, position by position, the former exhibit a smoothness of functioning that only long experience in playing together as a team can produce. Even with highly individualistic sports, such as track or tennis, team balance and coaching effort make a difference.

Dreeben lists two other cultural norms which the schools teach in preparation for the world of American adulthood: *universalism* and *specificity*. Whereas *independence, achievement,* and *teamwork* are valued attributes, universalism and specificity are not necessarily regarded as good features which people should strive to adopt. Thus, they are not values as such but cultural norms instead, which the school helps teach.

> To say that children learn the norm of universalism means that they come to accept being treated by others as members of categories . . . . [2]

Thus, a child in the fifth grade is given the same assignments as other fifth-graders and expected to behave in certain ways that fourth-graders or sixth-graders are not. Whereas at home he tends to be treated as an individual in a unique family with its own ways of doing things, at school he tends to be treated as a member of a group (boys, fifth-graders, Mrs. White's class, slow learning class, etc.). The standards of fairness and success against which his performance will be compared come from the groups to which he is assigned. Whether schoolwork assigned is too hard or too easy, punishments received too harsh or too lenient, chores to be handled too great or too small, privileges granted too many or too few, will depend on what others in his class, his age, and his sex receive in schoolwork, punishment, chores, and privileges. Equity or fairness means being treated the same as others in his classification. At school, as in the world of work later on, one is treated much more on the basis of how one is classified than on an individual, personal basis, as in the family. To treat someone unfairly is to deal with him differently than others in the same category.

The chances to learn universalism are much greater at school than at home. At school youngsters receive similar treatment many times a day on the basis of the group to which they belong: "Class, line up with the boys over here and the girls over there." "The A group will do the first two pages of problems in Chapter 3 for tomorrow." "All those who are going on the field trip tomorrow must bring the signed form from home and $1.50 to cover lunch and bus fare."

If Mike forgets his money the next day, he can expect to miss the field trip, that is, unless prior experiences with special school events have taught him that exceptions to such rules are often made. In each instance above, Mike has been treated as a member of a group and not as an individual. He should have come to expect equal recognition and treatment as others in the group for meeting the standards set for it.

As he goes from elementary to secondary school, i.e., from one or only a few teachers to many, he enters relationships which are increasingly narrow, specialized, and transient. He lives in more groups, but the sphere of activity and standards he must meet in each demand less total involvement, particularly in comparison with what occurs among his family and close friends. This investment of a relatively narrow segment of one's personality is an essential characteristic of worklife in an industrial society. The structure of today's schools typically assists young people to acquire this norm of specificity and, thus, to become prepared for the world of work.

What I have pointed out as far as some of the most enduring and important effects of school learning are, at the same time, some of the least recognized. One may find in the critics' letters an occasional complaint that competition is not what it should be in today's schools, but one is unlikely to find any mention of learning the norms of universalism, specificity, or even independence. Yet, these are basic features of the successful adult personality in a modern technological world, and the school is primarily responsible for helping the child move from the highly personalized world of the family to one in which persons are treated as members of various categories, each with prescribed sanctions and expectancies. If our schools were not organized, consciously or unconsciously, to assist that transition, our larger society would be vastly different from what it is.

Before leaving this discussion of the role of the school as a teacher of underlying societal norms, I must point out that some of them are changing. These changes, in turn, add confusion to notions about what the curriculum should emphasize and what the mission of the schools should be. In schools as in the business/industrial world, hard work, persistent struggle, and individual accomplishment have yielded their predominant-virtues status to such contemporary notions as "doing your own thing," "making a team effort to win," "living fully today because tomorrow may not come," or the economic credit-card version of the latter, "buying it now because it'll only cost more next year." In school, new themes manifest themselves in cooperative group projects rather than in common individual assignments, little overnight homework, latitude for students to choose what they will do and how it will be done, and relatively few, long-term, individual writing or research reports. The protestant ethic seems to be on the way out and with it the strong emphasis on independence and achievement motives.

Values rising in importance include (a) equal access to the "finer things of life" and education in particular, (b) cultural diversity, and (c) due process in the conduct of human affairs. Just as much of the noneducational litigation and social legislation of the last two decades has been concentrated on the rights of minorities, the poor, the illiterate, the handicapped, women and children, many educational changes have been aimed at removing the barriers to learning for those below the norm and at designing special programs to bring them into the mainstream of school life. Individualized programming, differentiated expectancies, cross-cultural representativeness, and the involvement of everyone seem to be the core organizational components for building a good school program today. What is to be taught is less important than how everyone can learn whatever it is. Making sure that the fruits of learning are achievable by all, in some form or other, is the modern educator's top priority. If all ninth-graders cannot read Shakespeare with understanding and appreciation, they might at least be able to enjoy seeing Macbeth performed.

Along with renewed zeal for opening the doors of learning to all, regardless of race, color, sex, ability, or creed, is a heightened respect for cultural diversity. Instead of schools serving as the prime melting pot for reducing ethnicity and assimilating immigrants from all over the the world into the mainstream of American life, they are to function as active catalysts for maintaining and even promoting the many ways of mankind. No child should be made to feel ashamed of his background. Human understanding can be enhanced by learning about cultural patterns from elsewhere. Where family roots were almost taboo as a topic of study in yesterday's schools, they have become one of the best starting points in those of today.

Along with the egalitarian values of *equal access* and *cultural diversity* has come a "legalitarian" appreciation for *due process*. The Buckley Amendment gave parents the right to scrutinize school records and challenge the validity of what they found there. Parents and children have won the right to challenge suspensions and other school discipline rulings when they seem to be unfairly or inappropriately enforced.[3] They have tried, though not successfully so far, to sue schools for failing to teach them well. Parents of handicapped children have won the right to review and approve, or disapprove, instructional plans for their children.

Proponents of the emerging equity and due process values tend to find their strongest base of support in the halls of Congress and the federal courts, where human rights have received the lion's share of attention this past quarter-century. Proponents of the older middle-class virtues, on the other hand, tend to dominate school boards and local government leadership. Part of the current confusion over school mission and function, therefore, can be traced directly to basic value differences among political leaders and to varying notions about the great American dream for the future.

Will America remain a melting pot where new generations of immigrants will gradually be assimilated into an ideal Americanized way of life, or is the emerging multicultural-multilingual movement heading us toward a new kind of civilization, a replica of the world itself in cultural diversity? Demographic trends indicate that Caucasians will become a minority population in California in the early 1980s, as black Americans along with those of Spanish-speaking and oriental backgrounds together become the majority. Will the society of the future have a widely endorsed set of cultural norms to transmit to the young, through schooling, and if so, what will those norms be? It is too early to tell.

Self-Concepts

What Johnny thinks of himself underlies everything he does and does not do. If he sees himself as a good baseball player, he tends to think about baseball a lot and to seek opportunities to play it. If he does not think he is good at baseball, he shows little interest in it and avoids playing it. He prefers activities he can succeed in and dislikes those he cannot. While other influences will also be at work, the cluster of attitudes he holds about himself shapes his likes and dislikes, his personal values and goals, and more generally his attitudes toward particular objects, persons, and events in the world around him. In brief, his self-concepts are the core of his motivational structure.

Whether he realizes it or not, he acts in ways that tend to maintain or enhance these self-concepts. Thus, he seeks out baseball situations where he thinks he can play at least satisfactorily, if not well, and he avoids those where he probably cannot. Who the other players are, of course, makes a difference as well. If they are close friends and his ability is less than theirs, he may practice extra hard to improve his skill or he may select one of the less important positions in order to join them; but whatever choices he makes will be heavily influenced by the concepts he has of himself, particularly in this case, as a baseball player.

Self-affirmation underlies much verbal interaction as well. While opinions may vary in normal social conversation, to some extent, people try to persuade others to agree with them whenever discussions are underway about politics, sports, or almost any subject. When they are unsuccessful in gaining support or agreement, they often change the topic, stop talking, or actually leave the group. People tend to join people who think as they do on various matters and to stay away from those who think differently. Such social behavior occurs, in part, as a way of reassuring human beings that their beliefs and attitudes, i.e., important components of one's self-concept structure, are sound. While one can observe the quality of one's own baseball playing and compare it to others', assessing the validity of one's attitudes is best done by seeing how they agree with those held by others, especially by those who are particularly respected.

Self-concepts, as with other attitudes and values, are the products of learning. They are the residue of all experience—at home, at school, in the community—not the sole residue but certainly a most important by-product. Self-concept beginnings take place at home, for the most part, and depend heavily on how much love and acceptance one receives. School becomes the first agency outside the home to contribute extensively to a child's emerging concepts of self.

> Since many classroom activities are judged in public, the pupil is bombarded with messages telling how well he has done and (with a short inferential leap) how good he is. If he doesn't take the teacher's word for it, he need only look at the performance of others of the same age and in the same circumstances. The school, in effect, plays on his self-respect. Each pupil is exposed and vulnerable to the judgments of adults in authority and of his equals, those who resemble him in many respects. If the child at home wonders whether he is loved, the pupil wonders whether he is a worthwhile person. In both settings he can find some kind of an answer by observing how others treat him.[4]

In contrast to recreational and peer group settings, the school forces youngsters to participate in various activities whether or not they feel ready. They lack the freedom to turn away from baseball, as suggested earlier, when it is an imposed school activity and all youngsters are expected to take part. Their withdrawal must be more psychological, more subtle than direct refusal to play. It may be manifested in lethargy in approaching tasks, lessened enthusiasm for school, lack of volunteering, slowness of response and other avoidance behaviors.

With some youngsters, aggressive actions—complaining, arguing, belligerency, etc.—rather than withdrawal will be the typical responses to forced participation in activities with which they feel unready to cope. Youngsters differ considerably in the ways they respond to situations which they lack confidence to handle. The pressures to succeed at school can become so great that self-destruction seems the only way out. A particularly high suicide rate among Japanese adolescents, for example, has been traced to the tremendous competition to pass entrance exams at the best schools.

Although teachers vary in the amount of choice they permit pupils to have in coping with school tasks, there is a good deal of forced participation throughout the. school day in a wide variety of activities—drawing, reading, writing, singing, playground games, answering questions, paying attention, and so on. Depending on how successful they have been in the past in each of these areas, pupils feel confident and able to take part again. For those whose early efforts have resulted in failure, especially where others have succeeded, an extra psychological hurdle must be overcome before successful performance is likely, namely, a negative self-concept such as, "I can't read but my classmates can."

The importance of early self-concepts to later school motivation and learning cannot be overestimated. Why many Johnnies cannot read in the third grade or beyond is because they will not really try. Early reading efforts have been so discouraging that all they have learned is that reading is not for them. "It's not something I can do." These deep-seated, underlying feelings about oneself in relation to school life cannot be eradicated merely by coaxing or urging a child to try harder. They have to be changed by altering the basic quality of school life so that a preponderance of success experiences actually replaces the patterns of failure that produced these attitudes in the first place.

The teaching formula is simple; putting it to work under normal classroom conditions with a wide variety of students is not. Let me illustrate how a mathematics teacher made it work with a class of low-achieving students in a large, urban junior high school.

Most members were well below average for the seventh grade, having failed one or more grades in elementary school. They were big, boisterous, and seemingly incorrigible. Standardized test results indicated they were at the second- or third-grade level in arithmetic, reading, and most other areas. Their attitudes, expressed in slouched postures, sullen looks, and defiant remarks, were, "School is for the birds . . . . There's no way you're gonna make us learn."

The teacher recognized that, before anything else could happen, these deep-seated reactions to school failure had to be changed. They had been stamped in by eight years of exposure to arithmetic assignments with seldom a correct paper or satisfactory performance.

It took six weeks of carefully planned teaching to bring about the needed change from, "Arithmetic's not for me; I'm too stupid to learn it," to "Gee, this stuff is fun; I can do it." Each day the teacher gave a test, had the pupils exchange and grade papers, and then asked for a show of hands on how many had all ten problems right, then nine problems right, and then eight. Most hands went up with the first two questions. He never asked for less than eight, but he kept an eye out for any pupils whose hands had not gone up on these three questions. He also never asked how many were wrong, wanting to keep the focus on what was right.

The secret ingredient in the formula was in the selection of test items. He began with first- and second-grade work, so as to be sure that performance would be successful. He stepped up the level only gradually to be sure that test results would continue to be perfect or near-perfect. The pupils never complained about the level of work, nor did the daily test procedure bore them. They actually expressed disappointment one day during the second month when he forgot to give them a test.

By November, attitudes had changed 180 degrees, arithmetic was a favorite subject, and the level of work had been increased considerably, always with an eye on the success/failure balance. By the end of the school year, some youngsters were almost up to seventh-grade work, the average gain being about three grade-levels. Sullenness was gone, dislike of school as a whole had mellowed, and what had been a "lost generation" was on the verge of "joining the establishment."

Admittedly, mathematics may be a particularly easy subject for using the formula because feedback regarding one's performance is usually unequivocal, i.e., answers are either right or wrong. Also, relatively homogeneous grouping probably made it easier to give group tests with the same content to all at an appropriate level for all. Nevertheless, managing an obstreperous, defiant group of 14-year-old city "toughs" is not the easiest of tasks.

The principle of ensuring a predominance of success experiences for each youngster is workable in any school setting, if one is imaginative in structuring assignments and has the resources to allow pupils to do things they are truly capable of doing. The residues of school experiences that become the attitudes one holds toward oneself are the most important of all learnings. There is nothing more basic that the school can teach than what a youngster thinks of himself, because it gives direction to so many other learnings.

Knowledge and Skills

It goes without saying that the primary justification, if not mission, of our public education system is to give young people the necessary literacy skills and knowledge to become solid citizens when they grow up. They should be ready to participate fully and well in the "American way of life." They need to read and write well enough to absorb and respond to the written demands of our society. They must know how to calculate and to understand and resolve the quantitative questions of daily life. They need to know enough history, literature, geography, civics, and economics to appreciate the common heritage they share with other Americans and the relation of our country to others around the world. Our schools' principal focus has been and probably always will be mass literacy of a high order.

The question to be explored here is not whether our schools teach the three R's and other basic knowledge, but how much and how well. What is it specifically that children learn and do not learn? We saw in Chapter 2 that many other agencies and institutions contribute to child development and the universe of knowledge they will gradually attain. How much, then, is the school really responsible for?

Since the publication of the Coleman report in 1966 and Jenck's volume a few years later, it has become fashionable to downgrade the importance of schooling and lower our expectations of what schools can do. I pointed out in Chapter 2 how little effect large doses of federal money have had on improving the relative test scores of children of poverty. There is little evidence to show that Head Start, Follow Through, and Title I programs, among others, have closed the learning gap between children of differing socioeconomic strata. In a few individual school efforts, they may have; in particularly well-implemented innovations here and there, perhaps; across the board and in line with the way the money is doled out, they definitely have not. The impact of many other influences seems overpowering for some children, regardless of what the schools do.

The complexity of school life has made it especially difficult to determine precisely how much difference schools and teachers in particular make, nor is it easy to isolate the factors that seem to be working. Education is terribly short of good research, especially in comparison with engineering and medicine; yet, its need for sound answers to pressing questions about how it works is certainly as great. There simply is no large amount of money available for the study of education as there is for medical knowledge or industrial development.

Nevertheless, several recent research efforts provide assurance that schools do have a lasting impact. Three sociologists (Hyman, Wright and Reed) re-analyzed data from a number of national opinion polls taken between 1949 and 1971. They identified some 250 items of knowledge that had been asked of people at different ages and with differing educational backgrounds. Knowledge items were focused on *popular culture* (movie idols, sports figures, etc.), *public affairs* (current events), *academic matters* (matters of fact in geography, history, the humanities and the sciences that were probably taught in the schools when the adults being surveyed were doing their studying), and *tools and duties* in four occupations. Examples of information asked were President Johnson's home state, the name of one's own mayor, the number of terms a president can serve, the length of a congressional term, Florence Nightingale's profession, and the definition of "edible." [5]

The most fundamental finding from this research was that those with the greater amounts of schooling had a wider and deeper knowledge of both academic facts and the contemporary world. This finding was true for older adults as well as younger ones. For a given level of education, furthermore, the percentage of correct answers among persons in their sixties was often quite similar to the percentage for those in their thirties. In addition, the greater the amount of education, the greater was the use of newspapers, magazines, and books, as well as attendance at movies. Thus, a hint of evidence exists that schools help a child learn how to learn. Incidentally, no consistent relationship was found between one's educational level and the amount of radio or television usage.[6]

Overall, this study supports the notion that education does indeed produce "large, pervasive, and enduring effects on knowledge and receptivity to knowledge." [7]   What one learns in school tends to stay with one and even enhance other learning.

A second kind of research finding shows that the more time children are in school and particularly engaged in academic work, the higher are the test scores. Because of differences among districts in the length of the school day and average daily attendance, pupils in some schools will have up to 50 percent more schooling than those in other schools. The amount of schooling available, as calculated from such figures, was found to be highly related to the test scores of sixth-grade children's verbal ability, reading comprehension, and mathematics achievement in 40 Detroit schools. The researchers concluded that "in schools where students receive 24 percent more schooling, they will increase their average gain in reading comprehension by two-thirds and their gains in mathematics and verbal skills by more than one-third."[8]

In another study these same investigators analyzed nationally reported course enrollments and pointed out rather extensive drops in overall enrollments in academic courses at a time when high school achievement test results were going down, i.e., in the early 1970s. Drops of 7-15 percent occurred in first-year foreign language, algebra, physics, chemistry, natural science, and U.S. history—the traditional basic college preparatory curricula. Fewer than half of all high school students now take an English course in their senior year. Meanwhile, concentration on the basics remained as strong as ever in the primary grades and may actually have increased during the same period. As reported in Chapter 1, test trends nationally were down somewhat at the secondary school level and for the college-oriented high school population particularly, but steady or even rising in the early grades, thus paralleling the amount of schooling devoted to scholastic tasks.[9]

A third kind of documentation of the notion that what schools do makes a difference comes from teacher effectiveness studies. Carefully trained observers keep very detailed, objective records of what teachers do in the course of a school day and how they go about teaching. They later analyze these records by trying to identify common teaching patterns among those teachers whose pupils learn the most, according to tests given before and after the instruction or before and after a school year. My colleague Donald Medley recently reviewed hundreds of such studies and digested the findings of those which were particularly well designed.[10] I will discuss his review more thoroughly later on (see pp. 101-106), but the major point to be made here is that teaching practices which have a clear relationship with pupil learning can be identified out of the mass of activity that constitutes classroom life.

I am sure that most people believe that how teachers teach helps determine what pupils learn, but seldom is there agreement on what those critical teaching characteristics are. Some teachers are flamboyant, outgoing, humorous, dramatic; others, quiet, reflective, yet resourceful. Some children seem to thrive under one type and others under another. Simple and well-validated formulas for how to be a good teacher are virtually nonexistent. Teaching is too complex. Students vary, subject matter varies and circumstances vary. What works in one situation will not in another. Despite strong opinions about what good teaching consists of, hard data that show what teaching patterns relate best to the amount of learning that actually occurs have been hard to obtain. The importance of the teacher effectiveness research, especially if it is properly synthesized, is that it provides solid evidence of what works and what does not in terms of how much students learn.

Despite reassuring evidence that schooling does matter, at least on occasion, and that achievement patterns are in line with what schools are teaching, the deficiencies in student learning have become glaringly apparent. What schools are not teaching well has captured the attention of the American public: the deplorable quality of written compositions from college freshmen, the failures of sizable numbers of American youth to pass functional literacy tests now required for high school graduation, and an apparent decline in the ability to handle complex thought. The Gallup polls indicate that the great majority of parents feel that the schools should spend more time on basic skills. [11]

Many educational leaders are responding to the public outcry by also urging a return to the basics. A distinguished panel of educators pointed out recently "that the distinctive role of the school lies in the development of cognitive functioning . . . . More specifically, American education should be paying much more attention to doing a thorough job in the fundamentals of reading, writing, and numbers beginning with ages five to eight, but then expanding the curriculum so that these basic skills are utilized in a broader, more demanding curricular diet." [12] The diet must be kept lean, the panel goes on to say, for children who do not learn the basic skills on schedule, to permit remediation and eventual mastery in the upper grades. "Otherwise, students will suffer from progressive incapacity to cope in a highly competitive society." [13]

Many school systems are well on their way to adopting the panel's philosophy, whether they are aware of its statements or not. Throughout the country large numbers of teachers and administrators are devoting long hours to analyzing the results of achievement tests in use, item by item, and to reshaping their curricula so they include more of what the tests require. While some educators deplore this "teaching to the test" emphasis, many children have obviously failed to master those basic skills on which other school learnings depend; it would only seem logical to assign basic skills priority status. Yet, as the schools have been given increasingly more and more to do, the time to concentrate on learning to read and write has undoubtedly eroded. After reviewing many carefully collected observational records of school life, one investigator reports that in some schools children are actively engaged in reading and mathematics activities less than 100 hours over the whole school year, only about 8 percent of the time that school is in session. [14]

One severe critic of our traditional education system and its rather modest accomplishments is University of Chicago Professor Benjamin Bloom. Bloom claims that by employing his system of mastery learning of carefully analyzed school tasks, schools could improve the capacities of all students to learn what the schools have to teach at a relatively high level. Instead of only 20 percent really mastering what schools have to offer, 80 percent could do so and individual differences between children would tend to disappear with respect to basic learning tasks. Evidence that his system is workable comes from a series of studies that show cognitive entry behaviors (a child's state of task-related knowledge) at the beginning of a course (or a sequence of tasks) to account for about 50 percent of subsequent achievement. Affective entry behaviors (self concept and attitudes toward school and the subject) account for another 25 percent. Focusing on entry behaviors and making sure they are in place before introducing new learning tasks should prove much more effective than our present system.[15] The National Academy of Education panel, quoted above, seems to think that Bloom's system has a good deal of merit, although it is likely to increase per pupil costs somewhat.[16]

To summarize this brief section, there would seem to be good evidence to show that our schools' efforts to teach basic skills and increase knowledge are indeed reflected in achievement test trends. Research cited here and in Chapter 1, under the test trend section, indicates that what schools teach is indeed learned by a sizable proportion of the pupil population.[17] What is learned has a long life, furthermore, and gives shape to later learning as well. With schools taking on more and more functions, however, as described in Chapter 2, the emphasis on learning the basic skills of reading, writing and calculating has lessened in recent times, and there are real gaps in the overall inventory of school learnings. Such matters as writing and reading need greater attention. We are still unsuccessful with children of the lower classes. New instructional models, like Bloom's mastery of learning approach, may be needed if real breakthroughs are to occur.

Greater attention may need to be directed toward what schools should not attempt to teach because of the heavy cost in time and effort that could be better spent elsewhere. Let me illustrate this point by identifying two types of learning they handle rather poorly now. I suggest that these types should not be considered as part of the regular curricular fare. The school is just not set up to teach either one well.

The first is learning to speak a foreign language. While schools abroad may teach English and other foreign languages reasonably well to their more able students, their cultures typically reinforce such learnings to a much greater extent than in the United States. In Italy, France, Greece, Japan, Egypt and many other countries, foreign languages are heard much more regularly on the street than in the States. Geographically these nations are small in area compared with the U.S. and have easily crossed land frontiers, resulting in much more contact among persons speaking diverse languages. Mastery of one or more foreign tongues is recognized as essential to economic and cultural advancement.

It is a rare individual who can go abroad and converse smoothly in a foreign tongue which was learned solely in our public high schools, or even colleges for that matter. The courses are typically focused on the structure and content of the language; speaking it is and probably should be a secondary aim. Understanding the written content and structure and being oriented to its sounds are about all students can expect out of two years of high school French or Spanish taught 50 minutes a day 4 or 5 days a week. Those who want more must immerse themselves in highly concentrated study in private language courses or actually go abroad to learn the language through direct, heavy exposure to it.

A second area that our schools handle poorly, if at all, is in teaching the essential work skills needed to get and keep a job. Vocational education represents a step in that direction, but in no way does it replace the need for apprenticeships in plumbing, carpentry, or any of the industrial trades. The best a school can do is to give students some familiarity with tools and a beginning orientation to the work world. Except for typing, which can be put to immediate use on other school work, business education provides only a sensitivity to the nature of office work and a few job-entry skills. Most of the learning will come on the job and in the context of a particular kind of business. There is no way that schools can provide more than a minimal orientation to the broad world of work.

Yet, major efforts have been initiated from time to time to close the gap between the academic and work worlds. [18]   President Ford was a strong advocate of this notion and helped spawn the career education movement of today. As part of career education, teachers are supposed to help children realize how that which is being taught is used in business and industry.

Business, career, and vocational education illustrate the expanded curriculum of recent years, at least when compared to that in the early 1900s. Foreign language teaching has been major academic fare from even earlier times. All such instructional efforts can sensitize youngsters to the world outside their homes and communities and can permit preliminary acquisition of some of the skills they might need in this larger world, but little more. How much real training they provide is questionable.

In conclusion, we need to establish clear priorities regarding what knowledge and skills schools should definitely impart to all youngsters and make sure they do this task well. Many other skills and knowledge areas need to be considered as optional only, i.e., to be learned on the basis of student interest, and still other areas need to be left alone for other agencies that can do the job better.

The Hidden Curriculum

A good deal of what the school teaches is not listed in lesson plans or curriculum guides. While they would typically indicate content to be covered and skills to be taught, they would seldom specify the societal norms or self-concept teachings mentioned earlier. These teachings occur more subtly but continuously, regardless of the lesson, as an adjunctive and partially unconscious component of how teachers manage classes, what standards they set, what judgments they make especially about children, and what behaviors they reward openly, condone, or condemn. Not only are social norms and self-concepts taught primarily in this unconscious manner but ways of responding and specific attitudes to support them. Educators refer to these relatively unplanned and subtly taught learnings as the hidden curriculum.

Teachers experience a thousand or more social interactions in the course of a teaching day. There is no way to anticipate the vast majority of these momentary events or to remember more than a few of them accurately at the end of the day. Much of what happens comes and goes so fast that guides and lesson plans are of little use except to help maintain a central direction.

Four hands go up in response to a teacher's question; which will she call on? Billie is looking out the window; does she call on him or ignore his inattention? Susie and Hal are talking and giggling together fairly quietly; does she try to stop them or look the other way? She nods for Jim to respond. Jim's answer is partially accurate; does she state a fully correct one, attempt to get him to modify it by asking another question, call on someone else, ask a brand new question, or do something else? All of the above might well have occurred within fifteen seconds, faster than the time it takes to read this digest of what happened. The pace of teacher decisions is such that there is no way for her to reflect thoughtfully about what she should do or even realize what indeed she has done except in a very general way.

Yet, from her decisions during this quarter-minute and many others as well, children have been taught such attitudes as, "You don't answer without raising your hand and being recognized," "You'd better not raise your hand unless you know the right answer," "Giggling and talking softly is O.K. as long as it doesn't bother others," and "You don't have to pay attention in class as long as you are quiet about it."

Philip Jackson, one of the first to study and write about the hidden curriculum, points out that some of the most important characteristics of school life with which a pupil must learn to deal are in this hidden curriculum.[19]   First, he must learn to live in a crowd. Schools house hundreds of people in a relatively small area, and his class lives in a "crowded room." If a child is to get along reasonably well under these conditions, he must learn patience and, more specifically, "to wait his turn." Whether it is waiting to be called on, to go to the lavatory, or to get through the cafeteria line, much of the school day is taken up with waiting. A child who does not learn to do so is headed for trouble.

In addition to waiting, children must learn to deny many of their desires. Of the four who raised their hands to speak only one could be heard if he had the right answer. Not everyone can be heard at once, nor can all requests be granted. Part of learning how to get along at school consists of coming to accept the fact that some of one's desires will have to be given up.

Interruptions and distractions are a third feature of crowded classrooms. Interruptions in thinking, discourse, and study come from many sources: noisy and disruptive classmates, intercom announcements, outside visitors bringing messages, end-of-period bells, and teacher directives to other students or for subsequent activities. Children who are compulsive about completing one task before starting another have a most difficult adjustment to make, because it is seldom practical for teachers to wait until every one is done to start a new activity. Thus, children must come to accept interruptions as a way of life and learn to return to tasks quickly when they are over. They must also learn not to interrupt others unnecessarily and to attend to their own work as if no one else were present, when in fact there is a whole roomful of other people. The essential learning, in brief, is to be alone in a crowd.

In addition to learning how to cope with crowds, children must learn to deal with evaluations and feedback about their own behavior. I have discussed this aspect of school life earlier and how the success of one's efforts, especially in the eyes of others, helps produce the content of emerging self-concepts. Routinely and regularly children receive evaluative feedback throughout the school day about how well they perform. Teachers praise but they also blame. Classmates too are both complimentary and critical. Work is graded and the symbols of evaluation are often displayed publicly.

The balance of praise and blame is not distributed equally. Some children seem always to be right, others always wrong. Most receive a mixture of commendation and reproof. While all children must cope with evaluative reactions to their efforts, not all do so successfully. Some adjust by learning to comply, i.e., by doing what the teacher says. A few do so by cheating and, thereby, getting better feedback than they otherwise would receive. Cheating might not take as blatant a form as copying a classmate's test answer, but merely faking interest in a discussion topic or assignment. In both instances one is trying to avoid censure and win undeserved praise.

Jackson stresses a third major component of the hidden curriculum, the fact of unequal power. Although children have already been exposed to the reality of adult authority at home, and with it the need to comply with the wishes of others, school provides further exposure in a less personal and more public setting. Whereas parental authority has typically taken the form of "Don't" or "Stop" to the natural impulses of young children, the authority of teachers is demonstrated more often in their giving directions and assignments than in curbing undesirable behavior. No longer is play the main focus of child behavior, as it is at home, but work and study under a teacher's direction.

Again the adjustment process is important if children are to be successful at school. They must learn to cope with authority. Most do so by becoming relatively docile and obedient, with their phantasy life remaining unchecked but under outward control. Some do not conform, however, but display their resistance in excessive day dreaming, lethargic work habits, sullen compliance or even overt misbehavior or deviance. Seeking the teacher's favor and doing things particularly to please school authorities, on the other hand, can lead to an over-denial of self desires that may be equally unhealthy and developmentally unsound in the long run.

The child must cope reasonably successfully with the hidden curriculum of crowds, evalution, and authority if he is to have much chance of learning what else the school tries to teach, i.e., societal norms, healthy self-concepts, skills and knowledge. Awareness and reasonable mastery of the hidden curriculum are equally important for the teacher. If the teacher does not establish fair and effective class rules and maintain good order and a smooth schedule of activities, she is asking for discipline problems. She needs to be clear in her directives, reasonably fair in her use of authority, and able to provide a good balance of positive-to-negative feedback for the majority of children. If not successful in these essential management skills, her class will experience much wasted time, chaotic and disorderly behavior, little learning and frustrating days. Those indeed are the complaints about too many classrooms today. Teachers who would attempt to improve the situation might well start reviewing what their hidden curriculum looks like and how it might be improved.

Earning Power

By opening doors to better jobs, at least until the last few years, those with college degrees earn from 25-50 percent more income yearly than those holding only high school diplomas. Those with high school diplomas, in turn, average about a third more than those with only an elementary education of eight years or less. Education, it can be argued, teaches people how to earn money. In the course of a lifetime of work, the differences between those with and without high school diplomas will add up to $100,000 or more, on the average.[20]

It is somewhat misleading to state that schools actually teach people to earn money. That is certainly not one of their specified functions. Our system of public education is justified on the basis of the need for a literate, informed, free-thinking citizenry. Schools most likely limit formal teaching about how to earn money to a few lessons within an economics or social studies curriculum.

What happens instead to affect later earning power so drastically is a combination of three things: (a) Education serves as a screening device for business and industry, identifying those with greater and lesser academic and presumably intellectual ability. It provides recruitment and selection officers with an easy-to-use, objective tool for limiting the number of job applicants they have to consider. (b) It also expands the overall knowledge and skill repertoires which provide a solid base for job success. Advancement in the world of work in a highly developed technological society is heavily dependent on verbal fluency and analytical quickness. Those who are most articulate, intellectually bright, and able to deal easily with abstract thought are most likely to move up fast. (c) Through the school's teaching of the hidden curriculum, high school and college graduates have learned many of the traits needed to succeed on the job: respect for authority, punctuality, dependability, and responsiveness to external incentives. The things that get one into trouble at school, i.e., being too independent, openly aggressive, or frank, cause problems for employers as well.

During the late 1970s, the economic value of an education began to be questioned and the income differential between high school and college graduates shrank.[21] With social promotion and grade inflation rampant and an increasingly high percentage of the teenage population staying in school and graduating (as compared with decades earlier), diplomas and grade-point averages came to mean less to prospective employers. The screening function of schools was being performed less well. As indicated in Chapter 1, employers found too many graduates who could not spell, or read or write. Undoubtedly, much of the clamor for competency tests as an essential hurdle for high school graduation represents an attempt to restore the screening function to public education.

The rising costs of college education and declines in the ease with which college graduates were able to find jobs, especially traditional white-collar jobs, also caused parents to ask if the sacrifices to gain an education were really worth it. Middle-class youths found that landing a job right out of high school was just as easy as for those who had been to college. Increasingly, they did just that, i.e., sought a job rather than go to college. Today, opportunities to attend college later (usually on a part-time basis) are often provided by employers for those who have become valuable to the business.

One expansion of the secondary school curriculum has apparently been of some help to job placement, namely, vocational education. In a major follow-up study of 10,000 vocational education graduates, compared with 3,000 academic graduates (without a subsequent college education), vocational graduates were found to get their first full-time jobs after graduation more quickly, to enjoy substantially more employment security, and to accumulate considerably more earnings over the next few years. They did not differ, furthermore, in conversational interests, leisure-time activities, or community involvements.[22]

Despite the recent concerns about the economic value of education, there is little question but that doing well in school tends to make later job success much more likely than otherwise. The odds remain heavily in that direction. Blacks seem to be one group in particular that has benefited economically from educational advancements. Whereas black male college graduates in 1959 typically earned less than white male high school graduates, black male college graduates (ages 25 to 29) in 1973 were actually earning more than their white counterparts.[23] Our education system remains a basic avenue to life's opportunities and the American dream. The farther one goes down that avenue the more doors would seem to be open.

Qualities of Good Teaching

I have reviewed what schools teach. I now need to examine what they do that works best. Of all that goes on at school, what counts most? The teacher? Instructional materials? Teaching methods? Learner's background and ability? Classmates? Grouping patterns? Motivation, or what? Asked in such a gross and ambiguous way, a precise answer is difficult. It depends on so many things.

If I had to make only one choice, it would be the learner's background and ability. In any number of studies the greatest single predictor of achievement test scores at the end of the year was cognitive entry behavior (prerequisite knowledge and skills) at the start of the year, not how the teacher taught or what the subject was. About half of all the variation in final test results was accounted for by beginning test results.[24]

Thus, youngsters who know the most to begin with tend to learn the most and know the most at the end. For first-grade reading achievement, initial vocabulary repertoire is a good predictor. For first-grade arithmetic, it is early knowledge about numbers. For ninth-grade algebra, it is fundamental arithmetic operations. It is this high relationship between learning readiness and subsequent learning that provides the theoretical basis for Bloom's mastery-learning model of instruction. For this same reason, many other theories recommend individualized instruction, which is based on careful diagnosis and prescription around the learner's state of knowledge.

Another major contributor is the cluster of affective entry behaviors I spoke of earlier, i.e., attitudes toward self, school and subject. When these are added to the cognitive entry behavior, up to three-fourths of the factors determining how much a child is to learn out of a given course are accounted for.[25] Viewed in this manner, the most the school can do, even with the best of teaching and the greatest of home support, would be to contribute a quarter of the total.

The answer to our question is not really so cut-and-dried, however. For one thing, entry-level behaviors are amenable to instruction themselves. As indicated above, these are the first points for instructional planning under Bloom's mastery-learning model and other diagnostic-prescriptive teaching schemes. I described earlier an example of a mathematics teacher successfully altering negative affective-entry characteristics of a group of deficient and defiant teenagers (see pp. 87-88).

Research findings, too, are not so clearcut as the discussion above suggests. Well-done studies can be found with different results. Jane Stallings of Stanford Research Institute reports that what teachers did when they implemented carefully-designed instructional procedures for Follow Through classrooms related as well to how much reading and mathematics children learned as initial test scores (for mathematics, classroom instruction was even more highly related than entry characteristics). Classroom attendance, independence of action, children asking questions, and task persistence were among the child-outcome patterns that were highly related to instructional procedures but showed almost no relationship with initial-ability test scores.[26] Despite the fact that entering aptitude is important and sets the stage for learning, how well the classroom play is directed, how appropriate the curriculum script and instructional props, and how good the acting (especially by the teacher in the leading role)—all contribute extensively to the final production, i.e., how well the child himself performs by the end of the play.

When questions are asked about which scripts and props are best, what kind of acting the teacher needs to do, and what specific directions should be given if maximum learning performance is to occur, research is even more confusing and answers even more debatable. There are very few universal endorsements of particular educational practices.

Part of the reason is the primitive state of educational research. The classroom is a highly complex place with much going on and many factors to be assessed. Paucity of funding for educational research in years past leaves us with an uncertain knowledge base for the teaching profession.

Only recently have we been able to study life in classrooms with sufficient scientific rigor to put much trust in research findings. A start has been made, through systematic and objective observation, to find out what really goes on behind classroom doors, what is taught, how teachers teach, and how teaching relates to what children learn. Although the movement is still in its infancy and there is lack of agreement on what is worth studying and how best to do it, initial findings are already providing useful information that, in some cases, disputes long-held notions about what constitutes good teaching and, in other instances, provides reassurance that what teaching is going on is sound indeed.

Several attempts have been made recently to review the best research efforts and to identify consistent, common findings so we might have a sound answer to the question, what is good teaching. While every person on the street has an answer to this question, the answer which these reviewers sought was to be based on solid evidence that pupils had learned as a result of particular teaching paractices. Such evidence was typically limited to changes in scores children made on achievement tests administered before and after a period of carefully prescribed and monitored patterns of instruction. In some cases it also included other objective measures of child performance, such as days present and absent from school, number and kinds of questions asked, amount of work completed in a given period, and amount of disruption of class routine or order.[27]

In the elusive search for the formula for successful teaching, I must say, first of all, that it is not a simple one. There is no teaching pattern that works effectively in all situations, with every subject, or at any grade level. Children differ, subjects differ, instructional purposes differ, and no particular way of teaching is going to satisfy everyone. Some patterns will foster solid gains in knowledge and basic skills. Others will nurture independence and creativity. What works for some (praise to low-ability children) will not work for others (praise to high-ability, high SES youngsters). The fomulas tend to be situation-, subject matter-, and even sex-specific. It is the mixture of several ingredients—teaching style, ability of classmates, interest in the subject, and entry aptitude—that really determines how much learning takes place. None alone will do the job.

The lack of a single effective set of teacher behaviors that always work represents the first major finding of the teacher effectiveness research. Let me now identify several teaching patterns that do correlate highly with achievement gains in one or more of these major studies. Given the complexities noted above and the influence of other variables, each finding should be qualified by the phrase, "other things being the same."

(1) Teacher use of time.

The more time students are engaged in academic tasks the more they learn. This is not only common sense but a well-documented research finding. Achievement gains in mathematics and reading are greatest in those rooms with the largest amount of time devoted to mathematics and reading instruction.

As cited earlier (p. 90), the quantity of schooling varies considerably from one school to another and even from one state to another; these quantitative differences make a difference also in how much is learned. Furthermore, the amount of academic learning varies from one classroom to another, and even from one child to another, partly as a function of how well the teacher controls the amount of engaged academic time. She does this by allocating a good deal of time in the daily schedule to academic work. She does it also by keeping pupils on task and keeping distractions to a minimum. There is considerable difference between one class and another in the proportion of time children attend to their work. Classrooms with the heaviest academic work schedules and those with the most student time-on-task tend to have the greatest achievement gains.

(2) Class organization and teaching style.

Another common finding that is probably explained by this time-on-task dimension is higher achievement where teachers teach the whole class or large groups of students at once, rather than work with very small groups and individual children one at a time in "open education" fashion.

This finding was particularly pronounced in the Stallings/Kaskowitz study of seven different types of Follow Through programs. Those employing highly structured, direct-teaching techniques had children who made greater gains on reading and mathematics tests. The typical teaching pattern consisted of (a) providing information, (b) asking questions about it, (c) allowing a child to respond, (d) giving feedback regarding correctness of the response, and (e) guiding the child to a correct response if it was wrong.[28]

I need to mention two other features of this study lest it be misinterpreted. Follow Through was established to serve disadvantaged children, many of whom had attended a preschool Head Start program. The superiority of direct instruction for imparting basic knowledge and skills, therefore, may be limited to the early grades and lower-class children.

The other feature of note was the superiority of children from the more open Follow Through classrooms on a test of non-verbal perceptual problem solving, in exhibiting independent classroom behavior, and in being absent less often. There may be a trade-off, therefore, between direct and indirect instructional techniques. The former would seem to work best for knowledge and basic skill learning, the latter, for promoting independence of thinking and action, and perhaps abstract reasoning. While children learn less in the traditional sense, they may like school better and think more profoundly in the latter situation.

One reason the open classroom children may not do so well in achievement tests is less overall practice on academic tasks. More time is spent on transitions from one activity to another, on interaction with classmates, and in pursuit of particular interests which may be only remotely related to traditional academic work. Academic learning time may drop off both when schools are too informal and non-directive as well as when they are overly authoritarian and punitive.

(3) Individual attention.

Although the most effective teachers (in terms of achievement gains for lower-class children in the first few grades) employ large-group teaching methods more and independent small-group activities or individual seatwork less, they spend more time actually working with individual pupils and they actively initiate contact with pupils when seatwork is going on. The less effective teachers are typically involved grading papers, preparing materials, or doing something else that keeps them apart from the children.[29]

(4) Questioning.

Asking and responding to questions is an important component of the teaching process. It varies in how much it occurs in a given hour of instruction and in the kind of questions asked. With children of low socioeconomic status, effective teachers ask more questions with a narrow focus. They can usually be answered by a word, a phrase, a number or some other brief response: "What's 3 times 5?" "How do you spell 'giraffe'?" How was Jim (a person in a story) hurt?"

They also ask fewer open-ended questions that require an analytical-type response: "Why are dogs called man's best friends?" "Why might Jim (a person in a story) not want to tell his mother what happened?" Effective teachers are not so likely as ineffective teachers to amplify or discuss children's answers. They are prone to acknowledge answers quickly with a "right," 'OK," "no, try again," "not really," and go on to something else.

Children ask fewer questions in effective teachers' classes. Such teachers solicit questions less often and are not as likely to listen or respond to children's questions as much as less effective teachers. They keep interaction at a low level of complexity and pupil initiative.

What is an effective question-asking strategy varies with the socioeconomic level of the students. With classes made up primarily of high SES children, effective teachers are likely either (a) to name the child who is to answer and then ask a question or (b) to ask it and then call on someone who indicates a desire to answer. The question is often a difficult one that requires thinking, not just memory or quick recognition. Effective teachers in low SES classes are inclined to ask a question first and then choose a person to respond who has not indicated a wish to do so. The questions are often quite easy and designed to give pupils a sense of success. If students do not give the right answers, effective teachers in low SES classes tend to rephrase the question or ask a new one of the same child. Effective teachers of high SES classes more often call on another child. [30]

(5) Praise.

The effectiveness of praise seems to vary also with the SES of the students. For low SES classes, praising children is apparently very effective. For high SES classes it seems less so, and effective teachers praise rather infrequently for right answers and often criticize for wrong ones. [31]

(6) Teacher affect.

Again the SES of the class makes a difference in what impact teacher affect is likely to have. Effective teachers of low SES pupils are especially enthusiastic and friendly and their children are usually quite happy. The evidence is mixed for teachers of high SES classes where effective teachers apparently display warmth and enthusiasm less openly. [32]

Teachers, and principals too, in schools that have higher than expected achievement scores, expect children to be able to learn despite limited home backgrounds and regularly convey this attitude to their pupils. This is one of the most consistent findings coming from studies of successful urban schools. [33]

In reporting these early findings, I should stress again that they come primarily from studies of experienced teachers in the lower grades. For research funding reasons, most of the children are from homes of low socioeconomic status. The major determination of teaching effectiveness are gains on standardized test scores in reading and mathematics. The research cited is also correlational, meaning that while things may vary together, we should not assume that one necessarily causes the other. Additional research is still needed.

Teaching patterns, as identified by this approach, are complex and interact in very complicated ways. What is successful with one type of class or at one grade level may not be at the next. Some research findings support long-held intuitions and common-sense notions about what good teaching consists of; others do not. There is utility in being able to confirm the validity of common sense, especially when in other instances common-sense notions are not consistent with research findings.

Nevertheless, a start has been made toward a science of instruction. The flimsy knowledge base for education must be strengthened in the years ahead. Let me describe the kind of individual study that can be helpful in resolving some of the many practical problems educators face.

Developing and Disseminating a Secondary School Reading Program

Stallings and her team at Stanford Research Institute (SRI) focused their observational research methodology on an all-too-common problem today, namely, high school students' reading deficiencies.[34] During the first half of this century, the poor readers never made it into high school. They fell behind year after year and finally dropped out of school between ages 14 and 16 to join the ranks of the *employed*. Today, they stay in school, for the most part, because to drop out means joining the ranks of the *unemployed*. The competency test movement has highlighted this problem. Numerous research and program development efforts are underway to discover what can be done to remedy this situation.

In Phase I of their study, the SRI team used a comprehensive observation system to collect thousands of items of recorded data on what went on during several hours of instruction in each of 46 classrooms in six California school districts. Their system produces simultaneously derived, objective descriptions of literally hundreds of classroom variables: grouping patterns; question-response-feedback sequences; amount, type, and source of talk; type and complexity of the content; and so on. Following the teacher-effectiveness research model, they identified several key teaching procedures that distinguished between those classes which had the most and those with the least reading gains over a year's duration. These procedures provided the basic material for the remedial reading program that was to be developed in Phase II.

In Phase II the SRI team conducted a series of workshops (5 two-hour meetings plus 1 all-day session) for other teachers in the same school districts. One-half of these teachers (the treatment group) were trained to use those key procedures which had been found in Phase I to correlate with reading gains; the other half (the control group) received training only at the end of the year. Observers gathered data several times during the year in each classroom to describe the kind of teaching going on. This information confirmed the fact that the treatment group was indeed changing teaching patterns in the directions recommended. As part of the treatment, data collected by the observers were fed back individually to the teachers on specially designed sheets which informed them how their own teaching compared with average teaching practices and whether they were changing their usage of the key teaching procedures as recommended.

Another major finding of Phase II was the fact that students in the treatment group's classes gained significantly more on the reading tests than those in the control group's classes. Thus, it is clear that the training made a difference in how the teachers taught, which, in turn, helped pupils learn more than they would otherwise have learned.

Information about how teachers taught was analyzed in relation to how much pupils gained in reading to see if the same key procedures were identified as in Phase I. For the most part they were.

Students made the greatest gains in classrooms where teachers provided much direct reading instruction and students were on task most of the time. Throughout the class period, these teachers were actively involved with students: instructing the whole group, having youngsters read aloud in small groups, discussing homework, and providing supportive feedback on their reading performances.

In rooms where less gain occurred, almost half the time was spent doing written work and another third of the time students were supposed to be engaged in silent reading. The teachers spent a good deal of time grading papers or making lesson plans rather than interacting with students. There was considerably more social interaction, disruption, and off-task behavior in these classrooms. Out of 300 interactions recorded in Phase II classrooms where there was essentially no gain in reading, an average of 51 were recorded when teachers were not engaged with students, at least double the amounts observed in classrooms where gains did take place.

Teaching procedures which were consistently found to be positively or negatively related to reading improvement during the two years of the study are presented below. Those positively related, i.e., happened more often in classrooms where students gained the most:

Discussing homework or reading content

Instructing—new work

Drill and practice

Students read aloud

Focusing instruction on small groups or total groups

Praise and support

Positive corrective feedback (rephrase question or probe)

Short quizzes

Those negatively related, i.e., happened more often in classrooms where students gained the least:

Teachers doing organization or management tasks

Outside intrusions (loudspeaker announcements, etc.)

Social interactions

Misbehavior or negative interactions

Offering student choices

Extensive written assignment time

Extensive silent reading

Extensive working with one student at a time[35]

I have several reasons for describing the SRI study. Others might have served just as well.

(1) It is focused on a very important educational weakness, i.e., the lack of reading ability among high school students. Thousands of teenagers in most large school systems and hundreds in the smaller ones can read only at elementary grade levels. With such limited ability, success in most high school subjects is unlikely. Without additional reading proficiency, the problems of daily life as an adult will most likely be compounded as well.

(2) It demonstrates how research can be used to identify successful teaching practices. Rather than relying on theory alone—or more often armchair hunches—to decide what should be taught about how to teach reading to deficient high school students, it identified teaching practices in Phase I which solid, empirical data showed were clearly related to achievement. A further test of the strength of these relationships was carried out in Phase II.

(3) It demonstrates how researchers and teachers can assist each other when mutual consideration and respect exist. The teachers had good opportunity to discuss their own concerns and ideas in small, supportive work groups. The feedback they received from the researchers was delivered in a specific format which guarded the information about how they taught for their own consideration

alone. The researchers did not have to act as if they knew more about how to teach than the teachers, but merely to present the results of research on teaching and let teachers decide how and when they would do what. The research data were put into a clearly interpretable form and shared privately with each teacher. Thus, platitudes and generalities about how one should teach—the typical complaint of many teachers when they attend graduate classes—were not presented in the absence of specific recommendations based on hard data. Further respect for teachers was shown in Phase III when the Phase II teachers were allowed to reverse roles and teach their colleagues.

(4) The effectiveness of the training program did not deteriorate when the research team was no longer around to conduct it. The teachers who had benefited from the training in Phase II were able in Phase III to serve as effective trainers of their colleagues, thus providing a multiplier effect to the whole process. The program, furthermore, is realistic in the amount of time, cost, and effort it demands. Six workshops in the course of one year is not asking too much of teachers or administrators, especially when it can be shown that they pay off in better instruction.

(5) Research documentation of the best means for teaching reading to deficient secondary students is qualitatively stronger in Phase II and III than in many teacher-effectiveness studies. By using an experimental design with both treatment and control groups being compared, one has a better scientific basis for saying that a particular style of teaching causes pupils to learn. Primarily because of political realities, it is particularly hard to conduct good research tests of program innovations in real-life settings and especially to obtain clearcut, significant findings, as did the SRI team. The complexity of school life makes the conduct of research on ongoing activities difficult, to say the least. Operation of the school program always takes first consideration. Getting representative, matched controls is often untenable politically. Stealing time from teaching itself to collect necessary research information is not usually welcome.

(6) This study shows good use of federal money. Along with numerous other studies, this particualr project was funded by the National Institute of Education out of its very limited $100 million dollar budget. Federal funds have supported other SRI research projects under Stallings' direction for over a decade. In

the course of doing these earlier studies, a magnificient observational technology was built up that was put to good use here. The complexity of school life requires sophisticated, comprehensive systems for objective data collection and advanced computer systems for appropriate and complete data analysis if the educational process under ordinary teaching conditions is to be fully explained. The research investment in landing a man on the moon is so much greater than educational research is ever likely to be; yet, the variables that affect what a child is to learn may be no less complex.

School systems typically do not have the kind of money needed to finance such research, and with most federal funds going into unproven but politically inspired program innovations, federal funds for needed research are in terribly short supply. It would be much better to cut back substantially on unproven program interventions and multiply research funds instead. An ultimate payoff in vastly improved educational systems would be much more likely than under present federal funding priorities.

(7) The study has many practical suggestions for how to run a good school. Besides the specific teaching procedures already discussed, the SRI team learned of a number of school policies that affect teachers' abilities to teach:

(a) Clear statements of rules need to be made and enforced consistently regarding tardiness, absenteeism, and misbehavior. Morale is low and teachers have difficulty establishing their own rules if the school's rules are unclear.

(b) Interruptions in the form of intercom announcements or non-teaching personnel (counselors, school paper editors, coaches, etc.) entering a room during class time to make announcements or gather information can be very distracting to low-ability reading students. They typically have more trouble getting back on task than other youngsters.

(c) Modifications may need to be made in the grading system so that youngsters receive reading grades and reports on the basis of their progress rather than their ability. Progress can be dramatic for a 14-year-old who is properly motivated and well taught. He may jump two grade-levels in five months, but still be only at sixth-grade level. To assign him a low grade after that kind of successful effort would certainly dampen morale. It could easily stifle further effort and progress.

(d) Teachers need to have their own rooms for teaching reading so they can organize materials and build a library of appropriate aids. Basic skills increased the most for teachers who had their own rooms.

(e) High school teachers of various subjects need to know the reading levels and problems of their students. They generally do not have the time to look up the information for the hundred or more children they teach each day. Teachers need help in having the information made available easily and in knowing how to use it to plan an appropriate program. They also need assistance in locating suitable instructional materials for the subjects they teach—audio tapes, graded alternative resources, etc.—so that they can make appropriate assignments.

(f) Students of very low ability should be assigned to smaller classes. They need classes no larger than 15-20; they need also to be grouped homogeneously by reading ability to perform best. High-ability youngsters seem to function well in classes of 25, even if heterogeneously grouped.

(8) Finally, significant progress in basic skills was demonstrated among previously hard-to-teach adolescents, given appropriate methods and school policies. There is no reason to give up on low-ability high school students. Careful research and sound program development can work wonders. Teachers, too, can change their ways of teaching under the right conditions and with the right assistance. Those who would give up on the educational system should be encouraged by what is possible when one concentrates the right resources and talent on our basic problems. The SRI study is not alone in providing optimistic results, but we do need more like it if the voices of gloom and doom in public education are to be stilled.

Promising results come from other sources as well as the teaching-effectiveness research. Whenever educators accept educational challenges enthusiastically and imaginatively, they tend to find new ways of helping children learn and realistic solutions to educational problems.

I recently read through a collection of 50 short accounts of successful education programs which had been started with federal funding. [36] Each of these had been evaluated by a panel of experts and judged good enough to disseminate to other school systems than those where they were devleoped. Together, these exemplary programs dealt with a range of educational problems and programmatic solutions: from an individualized Right-to-Read program in New Jersey for primary-grade youngsters, to a community volunteer tutorial program in Vancouver for illiterate children and adults, to a career education thrust in the schools of Cobb County, Georgia, to bilingual programs in Texas for children from Spanish-speaking homes, to special programs for the handicapped and migrant worker's children, etc.

In reading these digests, I became aware of certain recurring themes, despite the diverse nature of what was being taught and to whom. The themes included much of what I have already indicated are the primary objectives of our schools, namely, developing self-confidence and independence of action and thought, literacy and the basic skills. They also stressed over and over many of the qualities of good programming brought out in the research discussion above: (a) ensuring more success than failure for each child, (b) providing direct instruction either for groups as a whole or on an individualized basis with the help of peer tutors, volunteers, and para-professionals, (c) making instruction interesting by broadening the choice of topics to study, expanding the curriculum, using learning games, and taking field trips, (d) keeping children on task, (e) individualizing the instructional assignments and expectancies, and (f) providing students, in a supportive manner, with specific feedback on how they are doing.

One principle not mentioned so far is that of involving parents extensively to enforce homework, to review child progress, and to help plan his instruction. They can provide direct assistance in the classroom as aides or help supervise trips, etc. In some systems parents are requested to sign contracts to enforce various supervisory tasks at home. They are also required to come to the school for their children's report cards rather than trust to other means to receive them.

While many factors determine how well ultimate objectives will be met, it is reassuring to know that general guidelines for building good educational programs are reasonably well endorsed by the experts and, in many cases, validated by underlying research.

This leads me to the final question of this chapter: Just how good are our schools, all things considered? How do they compare with those of other times and in other cultures?

To some extent I have already answered this question. A partial answer was given in the review of test trends in Chapter 1. Educational accomplishments have been cited here and there in both Chapters 2 and 3. But only now, after reviewing what it is that schools do teach and some of our efforts to discern what is effective in the teaching process, can I give the most informed opinion. Because of all the earlier discussion, I shall keep my answer brief and present primarily new data that would help focus on the comparative question: How do our schools compare with those of other nations?

A Comparative Assessment

For years educators have lived under two false premises: (a) They are primarily responsible for what children learn. (b) Whatever children need can be best given at school.

The first premise was shaken so severely by the Jencks-Coleman reports that a reverse philosophy set in that said, "Schools make no difference. It's the home that counts and no matter how hard you try to reach children from limited home backgrounds, you'll never succeed." [37] The lack of positive findings from the various evaluations of federally funded programs would seem to support this attitude. So would Bloom's research showing entry behaviors (cognitive and affective) accounting for most achievement test gains from one year to the next.

Other research, however, points to the importance of schooling and the difference it can and very often does make. While the momentum of learning tendencies is strong and resistant to change, special efforts to alter children's approaches to school tasks can be successful if they are designed and implemented well enough. The SRI approach in dealing with secondary school reading deficiencies illustrates what can be done. On a smaller and less formal scale, the junior high school mathematics teacher (see pp. 87-88) produced similarly dramatic changes in what had been an attitude of outright defiance to learning. Even without altering entry behaviors, as this mathematics teacher did, what the school does account for is at least a quarter of what is learned, if you believe Bloom's statistics.[38]

As one considers the totality of what schools teach, there is no way of endorsing the idea that schools do not count. They provide much more than many people realize, not just basic skills and knowledge but a hidden curriculum of ways of adjusting to learning demands, value orientations needed for the world of work, and, most importantly, experiences that shape one's concepts of self. I hope that I have dispelled once and for all the notion that schools do not teach.

However, they clearly are not the sole educational force that shapes the man from the child. Home factors are important as well, as are peer groups, television, and other institutions. The school cannot claim all the credit nor does it deserve all the blame for whatever learning does or does not take place. The school, in short, is not all-powerful in its ability to establish and change learning momentum; yet, it does have a place in the network of influencing factors, and the role of the educator is to determine how it can best intervene in the context of these other forces. We have gone from an overreliance on the schools to a disenchantment with them. We need now to establish realistic, balanced expectations.

The second false notion that schools have been living under is that they can do almost everything. They obviously cannot, and they are suffering by being asked to do so.

Too much is expected of the public schools. They are expected by employers and parents to teach the basic literacy tools of reading, writing and calculation. They are also supposed to serve a job-selection function for industry and a minor league training function for college and, later, pro sports. They are asked to teach youngsters to be safe drivers, to eat nutritiously, to understand and control their sex drives, and to perform a host of other functions enumerated in Chapter 2.

Given the array of things they have been asked to do, it is amazing that the achievement scores are as high as they are. With time-spent-on-subjects a major determiner of how much is learned, teaching processes cannot be too bad. Some estimates of the amount of school time a child actually spends working on reading and other basic skills are as low as only 100 hours for the entire school year, 8-10 percent of the total. (The average number of hours, at least in elementary schools, seems to be considerably higher—approximately 130 for mathematics and 260 for reading—but still occupies less than half the time.[39])

The public and educational leaders alike are clamoring for more time on the basics and a pruning of what the schools have to do. Lest they clamor too loudly, let me utter a word of caution: The good old days may not have been as good as we recall, and school may not have taught as well as we now think.

Having heard his father grumble frequently about the poor teaching of spelling in today's schools as compared to those that had taught him, educator Bernard Faller found evidence in an attic trunk that his father's own spelling and punctuation in college English had been atrocious. The excerpt below was typical of the several he found:

In the distance a scortched (scorched) sign of chinese (Chinese) characters indicated a restaurant . . . a sweltering mass of frousy (frowzy) humanity wound itself in an out of cramped doorways . . . and into the turmol (turmoil) and strife of the city.[40]

Faller's father had passed the course, but he had not really learned to spell and punctuate until he became a distinguished newspaperman (reporter, an AP and UPI wire editor, and finally editor, publisher and president of the Colorado Press Association). Short memories and rosy views of the past need to be checked against the real facts which sound studies provide.

Test results reported in Chapter 1, for example, do not lend credence to the notion that schools overall are failing to teach as well as they did in the past. In some respects, they may have slipped a bit. Writing is a good example, but there are signs that renewed teaching efforts to improve it are already paying off. In other respects, they are doing as well or even better than formerly. Reading during the early grades is an example.

Black students, in particular, seem to be making steady progress. Between 1971 and 1975, 17-year-old black students gained 5 percentage points on an NAEP test of functional literacy whereas all 17-year-olds averaged only a 2 percentage-point gain.[41] Their dropout rates from high school decreased substantially between 1967 and 1972, and even though they were still more likely to drop out of school than white youngsters, the difference in rates was narrowing fast.[42] The gap between whites' and blacks' attendance in college is also closing fast. In 1976, 27 percent of blacks and 34 percent of whites in the 18- to 21-age group were in college, compared to 19 percent and 33 percent in 1973. By 1973, black college graduates (ages 25 to 29) were actually earning more than their white counterparts. Where traditionally most blacks who went to college had entered teaching, by 1975 only 10 percent intended to do so, the remainder shooting for careers in business, medicine, engineering, law, and other professions.[43]

Let me close this chapter with a look at how our system of education compares with those of other countries. In the early sixties a number of educational delegations came to inspect our schools. In good diplomatic fashion but undoubtedly with candor, they were quite complimentary. They praised particularly the amount of time spent on individual pupils. German educators were impressed with how much we were doing for the handicapped and with teaching about all civilizations, not just America. Even our teaching methods were singled out as superior to those at home.[44]

This was a time when the Soviet education system was receiving considerable praise because of Russian accomplishments in space. But Canadian visitors to Russian schools were unimpressed. They observed that Russian children started school at age 7 or 8, attended in shifts starting at either 8 a.m. or 2 p.m., and had an academic fare that was concentrated on the three R's plus early introduction of the sciences. From grades one through four, they average four hours of academic work. This steps up to five hours for grades five and six and six hours for grades seven and eight. The total number of years offered below college is eleven, but it is hard to know how many drop out after the eighth grade. Quite a few they suspected. All in all, the Canadian delegation was not impressed by any superior methods and felt that American educators could teach the Russians a good deal. [45]

Two things did impress the Canadians favorably. One was a weekly report card for keeping parents aware of how a child was doing. The other was a system of foreign language schools. Over 30 existed in Moscow alone, and English was taught in most of them. After the first grade, all subjects were taught in a foreign language, providing a much greater emphasis than in our schools. "Our guides through these schools were eleventh-year students . . . They spoke better English than we. They *thought* in English." [46]

Better than hearsay evidence and individual judgments about the effectiveness of American schools are the results of international education surveys conducted by the International Association for the Evaluation of Educational Achievement. Countries participating included Australia, Belgium, Chile, England, Finland, France, West Germany, Hungary, India, Iran, Ireland, Israel, Italy, Japan, the Netherlands, New Zealand, Poland, Romania, Scotland, Sweden, Thailand, and the United States.

One major finding was that in reading comprehension the top 9 percent of American twelfth-graders did better than similarly elite students in any of the other countries. Our number one ranking dropped considerably, as might be expected, when representative samples of all secondary school seniors were compared rather than just the elite. American schools included three-quarters of the age group while most of the other countries had less than a select third of their youngsters still in school (exceptions were Japan, 70 percent, and Sweden, 65 percent).

In science, this elite group of American seniors finished seventh. While this is not spectacular like the reading results, it probably is not too bad when one considers that we do not require even our most able students to take a lot of science. For that matter, our elective system prevents even the top group from concentrating its curriculum in any particular area because of the natural diversity of interests. [47]

Although the top 5 percent of our high school seniors made relatively high scores in advanced mathematics, American seniors as a whole had the lowest average mathematics scores among the nations tested. This finding undoubtedly reflects the fact that only a small percentage of American juniors and seniors take advanced mathematics courses. [48]

In keeping with the reading and mathematics scores reported above for our top seniors, even the SAT trend studies provide solid evidence that American schools are not shortchanging their best students. The SATs of class valedictorians and salutatorians from schools having relatively stable demographic qualities between 1960 and 1974 actually increased modestly during that period.[49]

Among 14-year-olds, when most youngsters are in school in all these countries, American pupils scored very high in reading. They ranked third with an average age-equivalent of 16.5, higher than their counterparts in all other industrial nations. Only New Zealanders and Finnish youngsters scored higher. Although American youngsters do comparatively very well in reading and mathematics (not nearly so well in the latter as the Japanese), they do less well in science and government.[50]

Perhaps American education's most noteworthy accomplishment, however, is keeping more children in school much longer than do other cultures, which permits a social mobility into the intellectually elite that is almost completely absent in other parts of the world. They make mass literacy of all our people possible, though still a sizable fraction of our young people have not achieved it. No other culture expects so much from its educational system. Whatever its failures, its successes are monumental.

Chapter 4

LOOKING AHEAD

American education is big business. One quarter of all government employees are in it. The school bill in 1978-79 was $87 billion dollars for the 43 million youngsters in public elementary or secondary schools.[1] Although enrollments were down 7 percent from the peak year (1971-72), the bill was the biggest in history. Education ranks first in government expenditures, amounting to 21 percent of all government payments.[2]

No wonder that school news is often big news. As taxpayers, most Americans have a stake in our system of public education. Those with children in school have a special stake. How Johnny fares there is a prime consideration. Parents and citizens are wondering if they are getting their money's worth.

Earlier in this volume, I focused on some of this news, that which captured such headlines as:

"Taxpayers Watch Soaring Costs While Parents Look for Results," *(The Daily Progress,* Charlottesville, Virginia (9/17/78).

"Another 'F' for American Schools," *(U.S. News & World Report,* 9/24/79, p. 13).

"Help! Teacher Can't Teach!," *(Time,* 6/16/80)

I have explored the accuracy of these headlines and tried as objectively as possible to consider the validity of the main criticisms that have been leveled at American schools during the last half of the 1970s. Under close examination, many of the charges are overstated; some are not. On balance, test scores have not declined across the board.

The SATs, it is true, did drop steadily for almost two decades. Much of the early decline was clearly attributable to the increasing percentage of teenagers with average rather than above average abilities taking the tests. Other factors contributing to the SAT decline were expanded curricula, more electives, fewer people taking senior English, changes in family life,and the distractions which followed in the wake of Vietnam.

Many other test scores did not drop, especially for those in the early grades. With overall test results apparently on par with those of earlier times and comparing well with those elsewhere in the world, the gloom and doom media portrayal does not seem justified.

Nevertheless, there is no room for complacency. A sizable minority is not achieving literacy. The fact that children of poverty, as a group, have never done well at school is no excuse. Because of our increasingly complex, technological society, it is more important now than ever before that all young people achieve minimal competency in basic skills. Undoubtedly our schools can do better than they do, not only for the incompetent learners, but for many others as well.

Despite the reassuring evidence of a job reasonably well done, the public has become aware of our system's deficiencies. Easy, rational explanations will not rebuild needed public confidence. Much confusion remains, not only over how well the schools are doing, but more basically, over whether it is even possible for schooling to make much difference. In Chapter 3, I addressed the latter question and cited clearcut evidence that schooling does indeed make a difference, and in a number of ways.

The voices of complaint, however, may not be stilled easily, even by the good news that schools are doing as well as formerly and compare favorably with those around the world. The seeds of doubt have been sown and the aura of confusion that remains will no doubt serve as fertile stimulus to further concern and complaint. The media's tendency to make stories out of things gone wrong rather than right will undoubtedly nurture additional confusion and complaint. It only requires a few failures to keep the concerns before the public, and no matter how good schools are overall, there will always be some failures.

The major complaints are over costs and the quality of teaching. As explained in Chapter 1, the cost complaints are not justified. Schools are scapegoats for citizen unrest over rising taxes and the horrendous expansion of big government. Because of its still heavy dependence on local tax support, education is particularly vulnerable to citizen tax complaints. Local taxes are about the only kind that citizens have much chance to influence, so they often serve as the target for expressing resentment against all forms of taxation.

The schools also bear the brunt of much expressed concern over general problems affecting youth: teenage crime (including 70,000 assaults on teachers), venereal disease, pregnancies (a million annually among unmarrieds), drinking, and drug abuse. Even though they are not the source of these problems, schools are viewed as institutions which need to do something about them. Thus, school administrators are forced to have policemen staff the halls and playgrounds of many urban high schools. They are pressured to keep pregnant teenagers in class, if they wish to stay, and to make special places for unmarried mothers who want to return to school. Absenteeism is high in many secondary schools (up to 50 percent in some), as are stealing, property breakage, and other expressions of our failure to socialize the upcoming generation properly. But the school cannot be considered the major breeding ground for such behavior, only a likely site for its expression. Schools are faulted for their lack of discipline, when in many instances their resources for dealing with it are extremely limited.

I do not mean to excuse the schools of some responsibility in these matters but to suggest the complexity of their task today and the reasons for public anxiety over the quality of schooling. Citizen dissatisfaction centers around lack of discipline and control, on the one hand, and the "perceived" downward trend in test scores, on the other. It is expressed in the demands for competency testing of students as a prerequisite to graduation and even grade-to-grade promotion. Resistance to tax levies and bond referenda and increasing enrollments in private schools are other expressions of citizen lack of confidence in the present educational system.

Teachers themselves are the target for considerable disapproval, presumably for being less dedicated, spending less time on the job, and being more permissive than formerly. They are criticized also for giving too few writing and homework assignments. Public questioning of the competency of educators lies behind recent legislation for teacher competency tests.[3]

Dissatisfaction about the quality of school life is not limited to parents and other onlookers from outside the system. Teachers themselves are leaving the profession in unprecedented numbers, as indicated in Chapter 1, and the joy of teaching is gone for all too many.

Fear of student violence is a key concern. It is much more prevalent, teachers claim, than statistics indicate. Administrators apparently do not report all disturbances in an effort to protect the reputation of the student and the school. Other reasons for low teacher morale are the need to "moonlight" in order to keep up with inflation, lack of administrative understanding, students who do not want to learn, incompetent supervision, and the decline of public sympathy and support. The complaints that teachers do not teach the basic skills effectively have been particularly discouraging. Over half of 5,000 Chicago teachers surveyed recently said they had suffered physical ailments from job pressures, and a quarter of them indicated mental ailments as well.

Public education is approaching a crossroads. Its future, as we have known it, is uncertain. Which road will be taken will depend on how various issues are resolved—issues about *mission,* issues about *governance and control,* issues about *financing,* and issues about *teaching and school life.*

While my crystal ball is not completely clear on how each of these sets of issues will be resolved, I can see well enough to describe the various struggles going on and the alternative solutions that seem possible. I shall devote the remainder of this book to outlining these struggles, sharpening the issues that need resolving, and looking ahead at what is likely to happen in the decade of the eighties.

Here and there I may make a prediction or indicate a preference of how I would like to see things turn out. Whether they will or not, will depend not on what I think but on what the combined force of public opinion throughout the country ultimately adds up to. My first prediction is that the present state of dissatisfaction, on the part of educators and laymen alike, will eventually lead to redefined goals and programs for American education, different patterns of control and financing, and altered styles of teaching and learning than now exist. Let me now restate the nature of the mission issues.

School Mission

What is it that schools should do? What should they teach? What other functions should they fulfill?

In the days of the little red school house, our society was quite clear on what it wanted out of education: the three R's and sufficient knowledge about American life and culture to sustain it from one generation to the next. In addition, the school was to assist the home in teaching respect for authority, dependability and other virtues needed to succeed in the work world after leaving school.

As I pointed out in Chapter 3, the protestant ethic and other middle-class values characterized what schools stood for until quite recently. Now there is a real conflict between these long-established mores and more contemporary equity and due-process values. The "melting pot" notion is being challenged by a pluralistic one in which multicultural diversity would become the essence of the great America. Basic differences exist between these two notions in both what is taught and how it is presented.

With the former orientation, teaching American history consisted of tracing the events where control was gained or extended over the forces of man or nature by those who were building a single nation:

<u>victories</u> over the mother country as we gained our independence, over primitive Indians as we went West, over those in the South who would split the nation, over those who would conquer our closest allies and destroy their cherished freedoms in the "war to end wars," and over those who attacked us and our allies directly in the second Great War; and <u>inventions</u> in agriculture, transportation, and communications that gave this nation a singular standard of living unexcelled anywhere in the world. The story of our nation was the story of the people who made these events happen and who brought unity out of diversity. It mattered little where a person came from; what he did counted more.

In teaching the contemporary pluralistic picture of American history, one is less concerned with the dominant themes of a single nation as with the contributions of the cultures and subcultures which make it up. One must attempt to provide equal coverage in the chronicling of historical events so that the value and dignity of all human beings stand out. The influence of anthropology, a relative newcomer among the arts and sciences, is obvious. The trampled rights of "native Americans," not "primitive savages" are highlighted, as are the accelerating destruction of our natural resources and the gradual pollution of our land, water, and atmosphere by the side-products of our technology.

Curricular differences reflecting the two sets of values, traditional and contemporary, are not restricted to history but can be found in literature, art, music, and almost all subjects. In far too many schools and communities today, lack of agreement and even outright controversy exist over what should be taught and where the emphasis should be placed. Communities have been literally torn apart by the teaching, before local citizen understanding and endorsement have built up, of such powerful new instructional materials as *Man a Course of Study* in lieu of traditional social studies content.

Even though these value differences contribute greatly to the current confusion over school mission, an even more fundamental difference of opinion exists. Until mid-century there was essential agreement that the main purpose of education was to provide young people with the knowledge and skills needed for intelligent citizenship and satisfactory career development. During the last quarter-century, however, the schools have been asked to do a much bigger job, namely, to correct many of our pressing social problems.

The most obvious example is racial desegregation. Beginning in 1954 with the Brown vs. Topeka decision, schools became the first institution that had to deal head on with the task of eliminating segregation from our way of life. Now, over 25 years later, industry, government, business, and other segments of our society have joined schools in this task. It is not yet accomplished, though progress has undoubtedly been made, but schools remain under heavy obligation to continue the struggle. Many of today's court cases dealing with desegregation issues still focus on school life. Few decisions over class grouping patterns, bus schedules, testing programs, and course offerings can be made without some consideration of the likely impact on desegregation efforts. Undoubtedly these efforts to desegregate the schools have drawn attention away from other aspects of schooling. Many would say, "What better use of school time?" But others would disagree with equal vigor; they would argue that schools cannot and should not waste time trying to cure the problems of society but preparing the young to cope with them.

Desegregating society was not the sole nontraditional task thrust upon the schools. Overcoming the intellectual and educational deficiencies brought on by poverty, so that children from poor neighborhoods would have equal access to advanced education and all the ultimate benefits it might bring, was another massive extra. Head Start, Follow Through, Title I and other compensatory programs gave schools extra resources to do the job, but considering the results, the resources must have been far too limited or the programs not well enough designed or implemented. The extra burden of running these special programs successfully and in accordance with increasingly heavy regulations merely added complexity to overall school operations.

With the passage of public law 94-142 came another gigantic challenge. The school's responsibilities were extended in depth, coverage, and purpose toward all handicapped children, not just those with mild handicaps who had customarily attended school. School administrators were now supposed to seek out all such children in their communities and see to it that they received solid instruction in environments as close to normal as possible; they were to intermingle with non-handicapped children. The ultimate goal was to see that these children would be able to function independently and successfully in adult society, despite the limitations of their handicap. Helen Keller served as one model of what could be done. The new law made it the school's responsibility to develop appropriate programs and pay the bills for educating all handicapped children to the maximum extent possible.

Close on the heels of 94-142 were the Title IX regulations which required schools (elementary through college) to provide equal treatment and programs for male and female students. If there were varsity basketball programs for boys, there should be similar ones for girls (or girls must have access to the varsity teams). If athletic scholarships were given for the former, the latter should also receive some. Women were to have equal access to engineering and medical schools and to other traditionally male-dominated programs. [4]

While civil rights legislation has affected all American institutions during the last quarter-century, the public schools have probably carried the greatest overall burden for implementing it and erasing discriminatory practices toward minorities, the poverty-stricken, the handicapped, and women. It is with the young, whose attitudes are still being formed, where the task should be easiest and the payoff longest. Through the public schools a degree of state control exists over a very large segment of our population that cannot be matched in other institutions. While commerce and industry chafe under an increasing barrage of government control and regulation, the chain of control is much less direct there than it is for schools.

Thus, the schools have become the major delivery institution for the "great society" programs coming out of Washington and Sacramento. It is through the schools that not only children can be reached, a primary target group in and of itself, but their parents and other adults as well. With the gradual erosion of family life, church influence, and informal neighborhood support systems, which traditionally performed much of the educational function, has come an expansion of expectancies of what schools should do. I will not repeat the long list of new school program elements that appear in Chapter 2. It is sufficient merely to restate that, for one reason or another, schools have assumed a tremendous array of functions they did not have a few years ago.

They have done this without any lessened expectancy for their traditional task of teaching the three R's and providing other basic literacy knowledge. Without longer school days or more days in the year, the amount of time and attention to this traditional teaching task was bound to suffer. And so it has. One researcher found several schools in which only 100 of the total 1100 hours of time spent at school during a year were devoted to such instruction. [5]

There can be no question about our schools having taken on a far more complex and diverse mission than those of earlier times or of other nations. There is also little doubt but that the efficiency of teaching children to read, write, calculate, reason, and become knowledgeable about the world they live in has been impaired considerably by their "social delivery" functions.

There is little evidence, furthermore, that the schools have fulfilled this social mission particularly well. Although blacks are gradually catching up with whites in the percentages who complete high school and go on to college, it is not clear how much progress has really been made in eliminating racial bigotry and hatred.[6] Certainly, the intellectual gap has not been closed between children of poverty and those without it. Little evidence exists that sex education, crime resistance, or venereal disease programs have had any lasting effect on the behavior of the students who take them. This is not to say that they have failed; there is just no solid evidence one way or the other. Driver education apparently works because insurance companies who keep good statistics on such matters give better rates to those who have had it. They give the best rates of all, however, to those with good grades. Apparently, the qualities that lead to good academic performance are characteristic of teenagers with good driving records.

Providing poor children with some nutritious ingredients each day through school snack, breakfast, and lunch programs certainly serves a useful purpose. So do the dental and vision inspections that take place annually and the polio and diptheria vaccinations as well. The school is probably the most practical place for reaching the greatest number of children. I do not mean to suggest that we should do away with all these fine activities. I do believe, however, that the number of peripheral functions the school must deal with today detracts substantially from the amount of attention it devotes to traditional teaching areas. By peripheral functions, I mean any activities that do not have clearly documented, positive impacts on children's learning.

It is time to do some curricular pruning. Priorities need to be set and decisions reached over what it is that schools should do. Currently they attempt too much. Their efficiency is too impaired to do anything well. Successful as they have been, they could do much better if there were a clear, unambiguous public mandate regarding which of the two sets of functions has top priority, literacy development or resolution of social problems.

Recent statements by educational policy makers suggest the former must take priority, for example:

> . . . the primary reason we educate people is not for salvation, morality or mobility, but for literacy, the ability to read, write, manipulate symbols, and develop independent means of making judgments and determining actions. In the past we were reluctant to argue that literacy in this broad sense was adequate justification for the educational system. Now we

devote less attention to the social impact of educational "outcomes" and more to the internal processes and problems of education. [7]

Although the statement above leans heavily on the side of increasing the literacy development function, pruning the school program of its social problems emphasis is easier said than done. Much of the latter is tied directly to basic constitutional rights which cannot, and should not, be denied and to a vast network of laws, regulations, and court decisions that have been laid down during this past quarter-century. I would not propose that schools ignore these basic rights or the legal network which backs them up.

What may be possible, however, is less pressure on local school systems to adopt untried or unproven categorical programs of dubious merit. Much closer attention could then be given to teaching and monitoring the progress of all children. Special treatment of children with particular problems could be arranged in accordance with individually diagnosed needs, not according to some artificially imposed group designation.

If bilingual programs prove more effective in teaching Hispanic students and others of foreign extraction how to understand the English language than immediate and complete immersion into English speaking programs, then bilingual programs should be kept. If not, they should be scrapped if for no other reason than extra cost and administrative complexity. So far, there is little evidence that they do work. A recent Rand Corporation study of the operations of four federal programs (ESEA Title III, innovative programs; ESEA Title VII, bilingual education programs; Vocational Education Act, part D of the 1968 Amendments, exemplary programs; and Right-to-Read Program) contained the following statement of findings: "The net return to federal investment was the adoption of many innovations, the successful implementation of a few, and the long-run continuation of still fewer." [8]

Behind the current mission confusion lies a struggle over who establishes policies for our schools. One cannot make sense out of this confusion without recognizing the vested interests of various segments of our diverse society and their particular expectations for our educational system. The chambers of commerce and employer interests want the screening functions restored so that those who hold high school and college diplomas have greater cognitive skills, broader knowledge, and more dependable work characteristics than those without diplomas. Minority groups have come to expect extra effort and special programs to make up for unequal status and opportunity elsewhere. They are especially sensitive to whether or not their children have equal access to all that the school offers and to full participation in whatever awards and recognition are doled out. Conservative, right-wing organizations and fundamentalist religious groups are bitterly opposed to the schools' encroachments on areas they believe are the responsibility of church and home. They complain especially about schools teaching values clarification, sex and family life education, situation ethics and other components of a godless and humanistic philosophy. College-educated parents want programs for the "gifted" to be in place along with good college preparatory courses. Local politicians and school board members try to reflect the community power structure and the attitudes of its leading figures. Federal and state bureaucrats sanctimoniously see themselves and their programs as playing essential roles overriding untrustworthy local interests, correcting societal ills, and making sure that laws are enforced. Like revenue men chasing moonshiners, they believe they have tasks to perform which only an outsider can do.

What resolution of the current mission ambiguities will ultimately take place will depend in great part on how the various power struggles are settled over who is to control American education. Let me describe the nature of these struggles.

Educational Power Struggles

Never before has there been so much ambiguity over who will control education. The balance of power is shifting between local, state, and federal agencies, between legislative and executive branches of the government, between school boards and community councils or boards of supervisors, between school administrators and organized teacher groups, between colleges and elementary-secondary school districts. In each of these arenas, interesting political struggles are taking place as groups vie with one another for control of public education.

Throughout the first two-thirds of this century, school superintendents were the dominant influence in local school governance. The chief state school officer had similar influence at the state level and typically friendly relationships with district superintendents. Federal bureaucrats were too remote to have much effect on how the schools were run. The lack of its mention in the U. S. Constitution gave the states ultimate responsibility for public education. They, in turn, established only general guidelines and left to local school districts the real authority to conduct school programs.

Traditions of local control over American education are deep and long-lasting.

Theoretically at least, these traditions meant local <u>citizen</u> control. In practice, however, most school boards, trustees, and parent-teacher groups supported school administrators and allowed them a relatively free hand. When complaints became too vocal and widespread, new administrators were found and programs changed. But the power of the administrator to run the schools was seldom challenged.

In recent times all this has changed. Following the publicity over test score declines, lax discipline, drug abuse, school violence, and all the other problems discussed earlier, the public became less docile or trusting of educational leadership at all levels. Schools seemed too important to leave to the educators, especially since they presumably had bungled the job. Schools, in short, became everyone's business.

City and county officials started doing their own investigations of school budgets, the major item in local governmental expenditures, and often made specific pruning suggestions rather than accepting whatever school boards or administrators recommended. Legislatures established their own study commissions rather than depending on state education agency (SEA) staffs. Governors and legislators became more active in proposing and establishing new laws and regulations for the conduct of educational affairs. Without consulting any professional educator groups (administrators, teachers, professors, or even the SEA staff), for example, the Virginia General Assembly initiated and passed a law in 1976 which would extend the teacher preparation period from four to five years by tacking on a fifth-year internship. Later, after they discovered it would require a substantial sum of money to implement the plan, the legislators rescinded the law in favor of more modest changes in teacher certification requirements.

Distrustful of SEA credentialing procedures in the face of complaints about teacher incompetence, a number of legislatures adopted proposals of the NEA and state teacher associations for their own teacher-controlled licensing commissions. Only in Oregon, however, (as of December, 1979) are these commissions empowered to act on their own, as organized teacher groups would prefer, rather than as advisory to state boards of education.

But the political strength of organized teacher groups is growing and is likely to have major impacts in the future. It was only a difference of opinion between the National Education Association and the American Federation of Teachers over the wisdom of establishing a separate cabinet-level Department of Education that kept the vote in the 95th Congress close rather than overwhelming.

The politics of education are entering a new era in which the mission questions raised earlier are likely to be resolved. Congress and state legislatures have become highly responsive to various educational advocacy groups as education has become everyone's business. The debates over education in the halls of Congress and the legislatures are loud and likely to get louder as the voices to cut back on tax dollars mount. With the increases in school district size and administrative bureaucracy and the growth of teacher unions and collective bargaining, individual citizens have lost much of their traditional clout for influencing school policy. Their best hope now is to try to influence legislative representatives, who in turn can be expected to be more active on educational issues than ever before.

The superintendent's hand is no longer so free. Expanding regulations and accountability reports use up his time and that of his staff. The collective bargaining of organized teacher groups, a relatively new phenomenon on the education scene, reduces the area where he can make management decisions unilaterally. Class supervision practices, planning time, bus and hall duties are among the dozens of matters where administrative prerogatives have been trimmmed through the collective bargaining process.

Firing teachers for incompetency is practically impossible. Lengthy due process proceedings and the difficulty of proving incompetence make it seldom worth trying. Only five tenured teachers out of thousands in one whole region of the state, were dismissed in the middle of their contracts with Virginia school divisions a couple of years ago, one for embezzlement, one for selling liquor to a minor, two for being emotionally disturbed, and only one for incompetence. Reducing teaching staffs as enrollments drop is typically done on the basis of seniority not competency, as occurs in most unionized industries.

Increasing dependence on federal funds burdens local school administrators with "strings that are attached" in the form of regulations to follow and reports to submit. The funneling of federal dollars through state education agencies (SEAs) changes the role of SEA staff members from provider of assistance to local school districts to monitor of regulations. PL 94-142, in particular, holds the SEAs accountable for finding handicapped children and seeing to it that appropriate instructional programs are in operation.

To the extent that evaluation reports continue to indicate that federally funded programs are not working, political pressure will mount to tighten the regulations and force local school districts to comply with the law. The heavy hand of Uncle Sam was clearly visible, for example, during the first year that PL 94-142 was in effect. When state reports indicated only 7 percent, rather than the predicted 12 percent, of the school population were identified and being served as handicapped, SEAs were told to step up their search-and-find efforts if they were not to lose federal funds. The threat of losing millions of dollars in federal grants is also what forced governors in four Southern states to intervene personally and establish closely monitored affirmative action plans in their colleges and universities.

It takes only a handful of complaints—only one in the case of court cases—to give politicians and judges the ammunition they need to establish new rules and restrictions in order to "correct" situations. Each year the Virginia General Assembly considers over 600 bills, a sizable portion of which focus on education. With each of those that pass, implementation and general monitoring procedures must be established. While each bill may address a good cause, one should recognize that a side effect of all of them will be some loss in the prerogatives and autonomy of local administrators and even teacher groups. One unintended side effect of the passage of Proposition 13 in California was the loss of considerable local autonomy, as well as revenue, with Sacramento becoming a major source of both relief and control.

Eventual control of schools will depend particularly on four activities, who conducts them and under what conditions. First is the financing of education, i.e., determining how education is to be funded and who will pay the bills. With local property taxes no longer able to carry the heaviest load, the lion's share will have to come from state and federal sources. School finance reform will stem from both (a) the need for more money than we now have if we are to improve programs and (b) court demands to equalize the amounts of money spent educating children, regardless of where they live and how wealthy is their community's tax base.

As important as the amount and source of funding is the type of funding and strings attached. Through categorical funding for specific programs, politicians can claim credit for educational thrusts they sponsor. As a result federal bureaucrats currently wield a much bigger stick over the local scene than the 8 percent contribution they make to the overall school budget.

A second controlling activity is testing. By demanding competency tests, state legislatures are taking over some of the control of schools. The extent to which they specify the content will determine how much.

The voices of educational criticism have focused most directly on test results. With all their problems, tests are still the most precise yardsticks educators have. If teachers and schools are to be judged on the basis of test results—hopefully with many other extenuating factors recognized—then we need to be sure that whoever constructs the tests knows what he is doing and selects the most essential content. If we are talking about standardized tests, it is the test publishers whom we need to scrutinize. Teachers and parents have not only a right but an obligation to understand the nature of the testing program and to question its appropriateness, because whoever controls the accountability measures controls the schools.

A third controlling activity is curriculum development. Who designs it? Who selects instructional materials? Who decides what is to be covered and how it is to be done? Who shapes the assignments? "The Teacher," one typically answers.

True in part, but there are curriculum guides to study, textbooks to be selected, principals, supervisors, and directors of instruction to follow. What influence carries over from one's college training? To what extent is the teacher really free to make these decisions and on what basis does she make them? Similarly, on what basis do others make these decisions?

One of my recent colleagues, Gail McCutcheon, shadowed teachers in their classrooms for several weeks, examined their lesson plans, and quizzed them about how they made such decisions. According to her findings, they apparently depend heavily on textbooks they happen to have. This is especially true for long-range planning of topics and sequencing of content.[9] If we will understand who controls the school, it behooves us to find out who really determines the curriculum. More will be said about this topic later on.

A fourth critical factor in controlling the schools is who is in charge of preparing and admitting teachers into the profession and selecting them for jobs. One of the basic struggles going on today is for the control of teacher education. For decades, while school populations were growing and the demand for teachers was always greater than the supply, nobody seemed to care about the quality of teacher education programs and how well prepared teachers were.

Recently, however, with the reverse conditions in effect, everyone seems concerned. In a number of states, legislatures have upped the requirements for entering the profession by adding extra college course work in various areas, more apprenticeship experience teaching children, and teacher competency exams as prerequisites to certification. Teacher associations have pushed hard, and with some success, for legislation to establish teacher-run commissions which would determine who and how many enter the profession and what their qualifications should be. Great sentiment already exists for teachers to control their own inservice education. They would apparently like, also, to determine what kind of training new teachers should have, thus challenging the long-standing status of professors of education.

It is not certain how the struggles for control of education will be resolved. School administrators and boards of education are not yielding the helm easily. They are still legally in control despite greater accountability demands and lessened managerial status.

The very rapid growth of teacher unionization with the 1.8 million member National Education Association now the second largest union in the country (behind the Teamsters) and the American Federation of Teachers also strong, would seem to make teachers a likely winner in the struggle for increasing control. A unified teacher movement certainly represents a lot of votes and political clout. With teacher cutbacks, however, as a result of decreasing pupil enrollments and tightened budgets, organized teacher groups have a major challenge just to fight the battle of job security and hold the gains of the past. Teachers have undoubtedly lost much public sysmpathy and support these last few years as a result of school strikes and strong union tactics.

Teacher leadership has followed the belligerent patterns of organized labor in many recent incidents. As a result, the image of teachers as professionals has been tarnished. Despite the union efforts, it is my conviction that the majority of teachers are oriented more toward what is right for children than what are their rights as employees. Hopefully, the conditions of education in the years ahead will permit teachers to move closer to the professional model than their current leadership suggests. It is not in the basic nature of most school teachers to walk picket lines or stump for political candidates rather than serve children and promote learning.

The resolution of all these power struggles will be determined in part by how the trend toward or away from centralized government control shapes up. If state and federal bureaucracies grow larger and local authorities lose more authority than now exists, as has been the recent trend, then administrators, teachers, parents and other citizens will have no recourse but to work through their congressional and legislative representatives, using whatever political clout they can muster. If the mood of the people becomes sufficiently aroused to restore local governance traditions with a considerably greater participation of local citizenery, a much different kind of education should result. Programs could then enjoy greater public acceptance than they now do because of the greater control by those most affected and because considerably less time would be wasted responding to directives from distant and unresponsive bureaucracies.

Lest I be considered but a dreamer, let me repeat briefly the story of a school which threw out the federal lunch program and operated an efficient, student-run one instead. Nationally the federal lunch program is replete with waste (over a half-billion dollars worth of food annually ends up in the trash can), government regulations (Uncle Sam even specifies the wording in the letter which notifies parents of the free-lunch opportunity), double lines in the cafeteria (children receiving free-lunches and those not doing so must purchase tickets which look the same, and then go through a second line to get the food in order to keep the cashiers straight on who is not paying, but presumably without identifying the children to their peers), and dumping into school warehouses a lot of unwanted food. In short, it is a boondoggle.

In contrast, a Pennsylvania secondary school set up its own operation, charging students just slightly more than the federally subsidized program. Students ran the program, decided on the menu, did the cooking and served the food. Those who did not pay, worked for their meals. One morning in the kitchen paid for one lunch. With the proceeds, those in charge bought modern cooking equipment for the schools and held two or three banquets a year. Most students working in the program regularly enrolled in a commercial cooking course. Several graduates pursued careers in cooking or food service. The community was delighted with the program.[10]

With greater autonomy and local citizen involvement, educators should not be afraid of being evaluated on the basis of how children are learning. In an increasing number of school systems, pupil learning as measured by standardized tests is being monitored closely and used to build remedial programs and guide class instruction. Parents have demanded and come to expect clear statements about instructional objectives, sequential curriculum offerings, and evidence of how children are progressing. A wide array of other measures than formal tests is also being made available for student and pupil assessment.[11]

When the new superintendent in the Indian Hill school district (near Cincinnati) took over a few years ago, he set up a large committee of parents, teachers, administrators, and students to sound out parental thoughts about what should be taught, subject by subject. Teachers then turned general goals into sequential school programs. Through these resulting programs children's progress was monitored closely and reported regularly to parents and administrators. Extensive remedial programs were installed to keep children from falling behind. A few teachers whose children <u>consistently</u> failed the skills tests were ultimately "counseled out" of their jobs, after efforts to help them did not seem to work.

Although the system is not without problems (good pupil records take time, less teacher autonomy, etc.), most parents and teachers seem happy with the results. As one teacher reports: "Rather than just saying we've covered it, we're saying the kid has mastered it. I feel I'm teaching more efficiently, with more direction. I have objectives just like in any other job." [12]

Teachers may resist such close scrutiny because they have traditionally had such a free hand. For the most part they have been able to close their doors even to school administrators and teach pretty much what they wanted, when they wanted, and how they wanted. By tradition, teaching has been a relatively lonely occupation. Like cooks hoarding their prize recipes, teachers have often been hesitant to share their teaching secrets even with friendly colleagues.

One result of parental insistence on both involvement and results can be a breaking down of this isolationism. Under proper leadership parents can become real supporters and allies, colleagues less a threat, and evidence of accomplishment much more clear-cut. While teachers may lose some autonomy by being made more accountable for what pupils learn, they may gain in pride and satisfaction by having clearer evidence and greater community recognition of a job well done. I hope and predict that the isolationism that has characterized teaching in years past will be destroyed in those ahead.

Alternative Schooling

With disenchantment over public education has come a flurry of support for private schools and other alternatives to traditional public education. Bills have been introduced recently in Congress and several legislatures which would allow tax deductions for parents with children attending private schools on the premise that they are saving the state money by not using the public schools. In May, 1979, the Supreme Court upheld a lower court decision that such a law in New Jersey was unconstitutional. With more than 90 percent of New Jersey's private schools having religious affiliations, the law in effect was advancing religion and therefore in violation of the first amendment.

The Internal Revenue Service has proposed regulating private schools, which enjoy tax-exempt status, by forcing them to provide extensive, convincing evidence that they do not practice racial discrimination. However, the U.S. House of Representatives passed an amendment in Spring, 1979, which the Senate Finance Committee went along with, that would prohibit the proposed IRS crackdown on private schools. Despite having only one-eighth of the total enrollment, private schools would seem to have the political strength to continue to flourish as one alternative to a universal, state-supported system of education.[13] Their biggest current curriculum thrust, not surprisingly, is a return to the basics.

Another alternative can be seen in the expansion of private business and industry training programs. Private corporations establish and run thousands of on-the-job programs training employees not just for particular job skills but in the three R's and more general academic subjects. The most extensive adult education activity in this country may take this form.

Private industry also operates tutorial and remedial learning centers for regular public consumption. People pay a fee and take courses. Control Data Corporation has developed a highly computerized training system called PLATO. Besides renting terminals and software to schools and colleges, it offers basic English and mathematics training, among other courses, in dozens of CDC learning centers tied into a central computer. [14]

Another emerging alternative carries the label of learning network. It is a nonprofit referral service for getting people together who want to learn about a subject with those who want to teach it. Credentials are not required to teach. All payment arrangements are worked out between teacher and student. The Evanston, Illinois, Learning Exchange is the largest and oldest of the networks with more than 2,500 subjects listed—harmonica playing, hypnosis, Chinese cooking, etc.—and about 30,000 teachers and students. Author John Holt is a regular champion of their cause, suggesting that for exchanging information and skills they are far more flexible and effective than schools. [15]

Under the federal government's Job Corps program, 48,000 teenagers, most of whom had dropped out of regular school, received basic education in 1978 along with vocational training and work experience. Control Data Corporation selected 100 such youngsters in the Twin Cities area and agreed to train them and guarantee graduates starting jobs at $10,000 as computer operators or customer engineers.[16] One controversial tactic used sometimes with CETA participants is to hire them on an hourly basis to go to school and learn the "basics" they missed when they went through the first time. Students who did not drop out may feel some injustice about others receiving pay to go to school. Another federally supported effort to help dropouts or potential dropouts complete high school while making the transition from school to work is Philadelphia's career intern program, developed by Rev. Leon Sullivan's Opportunities for Industrialization Corporation.[17]

These several federal efforts to help school dropouts find useful work and continue their personal development have involved the Labor Department in particular and non-educator expertise in general. Whether such efforts will ultimately be swept under the wing of regular schooling or conducted under the auspices of other government agencies remains to be seen.

Private career or trade schools, established for profit, represent still another alternative. While they currently operate under minimal state control, complaints that they often mislead students regarding the job market or push students through programs without teaching them, are causing state officials to reassess licensing requirements. During July, 1979, the *New York Times* ran a series of three articles on these proprietary schools and whether or not they should be regulated. At the time, 385 private vocational schools were licensed by the state with a total of 166,000 students, who paid more than $70 million in tuition. Subjects taught, such as beauty care, computer programming, notary public, and private secretarial work, were similar to those on public community-college course schedules.[18]

Many private schools also exist that cater to youngsters with learning disabilities, emotional problems, or other handicaps. Near Charlottesville, Virginia, for example, are two private residential schools that offer outdoor education programs—camping, canoeing, etc.—as their main curricular fare for rebuilding shattered egos. One is a non-profit institution and eligible to receive private donations. The other is a profit-making enterprise. Many of their students were referred by local school systems. The growth of such schools might well be stimulated by PL 94-142, which required public schools to pay for "appropriate education" of handicapped children in other institutions if they do not offer appropriate programs themselves.

Alternative schooling occurs more and more frequently within public school systems as well as in competition with them. Beginning in 1971, parents and teachers in a section of Minneapolis were offered a choice of four kinds of elementary schools: traditional, British primary/integrated day, continuous progress, and K-12 free school.

After four years of diversity and choice, 85 percent of the parents expressed satisfaction with their schools compared to only 35 percent before the plan began.[19] The options plan has been expanded and is now in effect throughout the Minneapolis system.

In Indianapolis, an options plan has gone into effect both to give parents diversity and choice and to desegregate schools. Seven options are available, six built around different educational models and the seventh to remain in the present school. Desegration is accomplished by using the percentage of minority students in the school system as a whole as the upper limit for the percentage of minority pupils in any particular option.[20]

Magnet high schools in many big cities are also designed around the alternative schooling notion. Rather than each of several high schools carbon-copying the others, different instructional resources are concentrated in each one to create the most attractive, well-designed programs possible around a given theme. One school might highlight the performing arts, another the business and commercial world. Youngsters choose the school with the program most suited to their interests.

One variation of this plan was adopted recently in Richmond, Virginia, by combining high schools with declining enrollments into administrative complexes. Students take the bulk of their classes in one building but move by shuttle bus to other buildings for selected specialties. High cost and low enrollment activities, such as junior varsity baseball or second year German, need be offered at only one location. [21]

Alternative schooling may well be a big wave of the future for American education. Given the present currents and cross-currents of parental concerns, tax payer complaints, educator uncertainties, and judicial demands, majority solutions for educational problems are unlikely to satisfy everyone.

The hundred-year-old near-monopoly of public education was shaken in its roots by the introduction of voucher plans a few years ago and, more recently, by tuition tax credits to help send children to private schools. It took a massive lobbying effort by the National PTA, the NEA, and a broad coalition of labor, civil rights, education, religious, and civic organizations to defeat the tuition tax-credit legislation on a close vote in the ninety-sixth Congress. What will happen in the ninety-seventh remains to be seen.

The strength of those opposing the continuance of a single system of public education could well grow in the years ahead if educators are not more responsive than they have been to parental desires. Parents including minorities, who can afford to use the private schools do so for many reasons: a sincere desire for an education based on religious values, disruptions and distraction brought about by desegregation and other expanded mission activities, violence and crime which are augumented by the size and impersonality of big schools, the lack of personal influence and involvement in the education of their children, and disagreement with the perceived philosophy of education in effect. Two authorities state the reasons as follows:

> Far too many parents far too often feel themselves to be at the mercy of a remote and unresponsive bureaucracy . . . . Parents are rarely if ever consulted about what they want for their children. They are rarely given an opportunity first to define and then to select the kind of schooling they want. Given little diversity and almost no choice within the public system, parents are pushed toward exercising the only choice they have, the choice of abandoning the public schools altogether. [22]

The educational establishment has been challenged as never before. It is by no means certain that it can get its act together fast enough and provide the diversity, choice, quality, and involvement that are being demanded before other forces succeed in destroying the universal system of public education as we have known it during this century. The moves in Minneapolis, Richmond, and Indianapolis are in the right direction to save the public schools. In the latter, some private school parents have opted back to the public system now that choices are available.

Whether or not the educational establishment succeeds depends also on how the various power struggles are resolved and whether certain partisan forces can start working together to improve the quality of schooling. It is to this important topic that I now turn.

Schooling in 1990

What will schools be like a decade hence or at the turn of the century? How will they differ from those of today? Will the public education mission be narrower and clearer? If so, what other institutions will be picking up remaining responsibilities? Will schooling be more or less effective than it is now?

In dealing with questions such as these, I change from reporter and analyst of our educational condition to editor and prognosticator of its future. Whereas I have tried to keep personal biases about what's good for education somewhat under control in reporting the educational condition, I intend to expose them fully as I look ahead at what schools could be like.

Those who do not want to read the editorial but just the news, should close this volume right here. Those who want to look ahead and reflect on conjecture may plod on.

In looking ahead, I intend to stress what I would like to see happen more than trying to predict what is most likely to occur. Attempted clairvoyance regarding the most likely resolution of the several power struggles and mission debates is not particularly useful at this stage of analysis. I would like to think that we can intervene in the political process sufficiently to help determine the kinds of schools we will have and the outcome of the various power struggles. While the forces that would shape education are numerous and formidable, they are not yet set in concrete. To a considerable extent the public can have the kinds of schools it wants. What I shall try to do, therefore, is to make my arguments so convincing that readers might actually wish to stump in their own localities for certain notions about how schools should be run.

Because I am not identifying the most probable happenings, one should not assume that the ideas presented are unrealistic fancies and utopian plans, the phantasies of an "ivy-tower professor." Based on the research already reviewed, the major principles suggested about schooling seem workable and realistic. Reasons will be cited as they are presented.

1. *Organization* —School units will be considerably smaller, more autonomously administered, more personal, and more narrowly focused in instructional themes and patterns.* Comprehensive high schools will yield to a wide variety of smaller schools, each reflecting a somewhat different instructional emphasis (e.g., performing arts, biological sciences, basic skills and coordinated work experience), scheduling patterns and teaching styles. Even if the same buildings are used, they will be divided into sections (mini-schools) of semi-autonomous clusters with 100-300 people—pupils, teachers, aides, and resource specialists—in each. The teaching staff will tend to recognize all children and parents, not just those they teach. Teachers, parents, and children will all have some choice of schools and programs, with sufficient constraints so as to ensure community representativeness in socioeconomic and racial makeup.

---

* Unless otherwise specified, all comparisons are with the present condition.

Rationale: Smaller organizational units would (a) allow greater participation by all in the development of rules and regulations, (b) nurture more institutional loyalty, (c) cut back on the overall bureaucracy, (d) foster closer personal relationships between all people in the school community, (e) spread the active as contrasted with onlooker involvement of students in all activities, (f) prevent youngsters from being overlooked or ignored, (g) provide closer monitoring of learning progress and student behavior, and (h) minimize disruptive classroom or corridor activity. Alternative schools report less truancy, less vandalism and violence, and fewer absences of teachers as well as students than comparable schools in the same districts. [23]

The "rebirth" of Brooklyn's Wingate High School illustrates how the mini-school approach can be used both to provide special instruction for clearly identified target populations and to initiate overall curricular reform throughout the institution. In one thrust, the best young, dedicated teachers were selected to work intensively with the poorest students on their basic skills. In another, instead of providing a bilingual education for a sizable group of French-speaking students from Haiti, the principal established a program of total immersion in the English language. As the students in these programs began to learn, disruption declined and attention was turned to revamping the rest of the curriculum. [24]

Since no teaching style or school organizational pattern has been found superior at all grade levels for all kinds of students and all purposes, provision of diversity and choice seems the most realistic way of meeting the wide range of parental, child, and teacher expectations. People can select those which best match their overall preferences. The child who goes berserk in nonstructured situations should not end up in an open school and vice versa, one who blooms under such conditions should have them. Parental satisfaction should improve as well.

2.   *Administration*—Responsibility for the teaching program will rest primarily on the shoulders of head teachers (teaching principals) in these smaller schools or mini-schools. They will be held accountable to district-wide administrators for ensuring that legal and fiscal requirements are met, and for satisfying community expectations. They will be accountable directly to parents for meeting program expectations for children. If they fail to do so, parents can choose other alternatives for their children, or if these are not available, they can ask district administrators to provide better alternatives.

District-wide administrators will be fewer in number and have less direct program responsibility. Their main instructional responsibility will be to ensure that sufficient choices are available. After that, they will generally be in a position of supporting head teachers, providing them with maximum resources, and handling the business side of school operations with a minimum of interference to classroom instruction.

Within a school or mini-school, head teachers will select and supervise the staff and administer the overall instructional program. They will have the obligation of designing instructional programs that clearly specify how teaching will be conducted, how time at school will be allocated among subjects and activities, what pupils can be expected to learn, and what measures will be used to determine how well objectives are being met. At the high school levels especially, they will also coordinate building activities with instructional components scheduled elsewhere, i.e., in other school buildings, in other agencies, in the community at large, or at work sites. They will have to deal effectively with community councils, solicit parental curriculum input and reaction to school programs and child progress, and assume responsibility for all that goes on.

Rationale: Sound programs emerge from people with vision and maturity, but also control and clout. The responsibility for developing and running a good program will rest with those in closest contact with the customer to be satisfied. Red tape and bureaucratic layers of authority must be removed from the daily operation of the school program if instructional time-on-task is to improve and teachers are to have time to teach. Ultimate accountability will be to the clients who have chosen each particular school.

Schools will have to become more responsive. The bigness and diffuse authority of today's schools leave no one accountable in a precise way. Current layers of bureaucracy make it difficult for broad segments of the community to contact people who are in a position to make changes. In a smaller, autonomously run school, rules and programs can be changed, if they do not work, through direct contact with the people involved.

Considerable recent research indicates that how individual schools are administered determines in part how much learning takes place, even in poverty neighborhoods. Effective schools where children's achievement scores are higher than socioeconomic factors would predict tend to have one or more of the following characteristics: principals who constantly prod teachers to have all youngsters master basic skills at least at minimal levels, greater faculty and staff expectations that children can learn, more time devoted to direct instruction, an orderly and task-oriented class atmosphere, more support services from the central administration, and greater teacher job satisfaction.[25] A groundswell of citizen feeling is sweeping the country that schools should be much more precise in stating what they are doing instructionally and what their learning objectives are, and in providing data to show how well they are meeting those objectives. To a much greater extent then ever before, administrators and teachers are being held accountable for producing reasonable results.

3.   *Parental and Community Involvement*—Parents will be much more actively involved in the education of their children. They will have a choice in which schools their children attend. They will have opportunity to participate in curriculum planning and to serve on instructional teams as volunteer or paid aides. They will receive frequently rather precise reports of their children's progress. They will be informed about homework assignments, and they will be expected to monitor home study time. Much closer personal relationships will exist between home and school. Teachers will be held directly accountable to the parents and citizens who are their patrons.

Some of the smaller, more specialized units that will replace today's comprehensive high schools will provide components of youngsters' education in the workplace itself. In Hartford, Connecticut, for example, carefully selected juniors and seniors spend half of each day at one of four career education centers taking job-related academic classes and the other half working at one of the sponsoring companies. The school system collaborated with several dozen companies and agencies to establish career centers for insurance and banking, electro-mechanical positions, auto-mechanical jobs, and health care employment.[26]

Overall, schools of the future can be expected to utilize community resources—institutional and human—much more extensively than in the past. The creator of the Foxfire movement, Eliot Wigginton states:

> . . . students and teachers must be engaged directly with the community at large forging two-way relationships that not only educate, but endure and make a difference in the quality of life. One of the most distressing facts I encounter in every school I work with is how ignorant teachers are of the community from which their students are drawn.[27]

John Goodlad even proposes allocating vouchers to obtain out-of-school personnel resources to cultivate special interests of youngsters.[28]

Rationale: Until recently, schooling in this country was always a local affair. Local lay control is a deeply rooted tradition in American education. Local school boards and not state or federal authorities still have the final legal responsibility for the operation of the American schools.

As a result of community growth and school district consolidation, school systems have expanded in size many times with an accompanying loss of local citizen involvement, especially at the individual building level. Home support and contact have become remote due to the bigness and impersonality of the schools and changes in family living patterns. For one reason or another, homes have been left with less and less responsibility, schools with more and more.

These patterns must be reversed, as is beginning to happen in numerous localities where parents are being asked to monitor home study daily and communicate regularly with the school about such efforts. Such traditional patterns of home-school cooperation are being put into practice in a number of heavily populated urban areas where both parents work.

Strong arguments can be made for parent advisory groups or school-site councils for each building made up of parents, teachers, and even students. They should actually have the authority to target or withhold funds, not just advise.[29] In places where court-ordered desegregation plans are in effect, judges have frequently established citizens councils, in order to monitor their implementation and make progress reports to the courts. Public law 94-142 decrees parental involvement and formal acceptance of written instructional plans for each handicapped child.

Although legal mandates may often be in force, the real reasons that schools need to involve parents more directly is to strengthen the instructional process. Teachers cannot do their job well without knowing a lot about their pupils, much of which only parents can tell them, and without having home reinforcement and support as well. Teachers need to have their own perceptions sharpened by hearing what parents think. Head Start and Follow Through programs that have been most successful in producing achievement gains in the basic skills included those models with the greatest amount of parent involvement. One of the Coleman report's undisputed findings was higher achievement scores in schools with active PTAs, all other things being equal.[30]

One final reason is the need for coordinating child services. If some cutback occurs in the direct use of schools for delivering health, nutritional, dental, and social services, the school still needs to be aware of what services children are receiving and how it can best fit into the overall network of community agencies and home resources. Parents and teachers need to know each other, respect each other, and share needed information regularly, if children's schooling is to work best.

The use of aides and paraprofessionals is one way to expand the overall staff at minimal cost, relieve teachers of burdensome and energy-draining chores, and increase the number of adults available for child management and tutoring activities. Such persons have proved helpful in working with individual students, designing bulletin boards and art projects, doing clerical work, supervising field trips, and performing dozens of other tasks relevant to their abilities.[31] Recent Gallup Polls indicate that a large majority of Americans over sixty are willing to give some time to volunteer activities, but only a handful have ever been asked.

4.   *Mission*—The mission will clearly make literacy development the number one function. The goal will be to help the entire student population develop the skills and knowledge necessary to participate fully in our society when they become adult citizens. All other functions, including desegregating society, running a minor league sports program, and trying to minister to the health/nutrition needs of the poor, will be subordinate to the main mission. To the extent that subordinate functions complicate attainment of the principal school task, they will be given to other agencies to do.

Rationale: The schools have had far too many tasks in recent years besides teaching pupils to read, write, calculate, reason, and become informed about the country and world they live in. If children learn these things well so that the principal mission is achieved, many of the other current functions would be taken care of also; at least the school would have done all it could to help with such functions. If a child learns well what the school has to teach, for example, he will have gone a long way toward developing the self-assurance and other necessary qualifications to meet the job-entry level satisfactorily. He undoubtedly will also have learned the essential hidden curricula well enough to cope with the frustrations of today's living and working patterns.

Not only have schools been diverted from their primary mission by having to assume too many other duties, but they have also lost any semblance of a core curriculum for all students. Programs vary so much today that only 16 specific courses are offered in 50 percent or more of the nation's high schools, including band, chorus, driver education, and typing.[32] The alternative programming I propose would not change this mishmash of diverse curriucla across the entire schooling spectrum. Choice would still remain a prime feature from one situation to the next and even within school classrooms. But within each of the smaller administrative units of the future, a more carefully integrated and clearly specified pattern of instructional style and emphasis would prevail. Despite the choices and diversity, functional literacy would serve as the overarching planning aim and subsequent evaluation criterion.

The task of teaching 100 percent of the youngsters to be functionally literate in such a high technology society is itself formidable. People have not yet even agreed on what literacy is. Is it fourth-, sixth-, or eighth-grade scores? Real-life reading tasks vary greatly. The reading difficulty of many popular magazines has been pegged at the twelfth-grade level *(Popular Mechanics, Ladies Home Journal, Readers Digest)*. Studies of army personnel show that cooks need ninth-grade reading skills to understand their technical manuals, repairmen fourteenth-grade skills, and supply specialists sixteenth-year ability, the same as that required by college professors.[33]

Where some standards are expressed as averages on standardized tests, others are designed as direct measures of the ability to handle current life tasks. Maryland competency tests, for example, contain five kinds of items: (a) *following directions,* with selections from cooking, sewing, and first aid materials; (b) *locating references* from trade books, consumer guides, and atlases; (c) *gaining information* from "want ads," legal documents, and training manuals; (d) *understanding forms* such as income-tax forms, leases, and applications; and (e) *attaining personal development,* a rating of personal reading habits.[34]

In the mathematics area how much understanding of symbolic logic and quantitative relationships will be necessary for the world of tomorrow? How much familiarity should there be with the computer and other emerging tools for solving the vast data-oriented problems of our society?

Currently, there is much concern over a recent report to the President on the condition of science and engineering education in this country. It indicates, among other matters, that 5 million Soviet youths take calculus during secondary school each year compared to only 500 thousand Americans, who take it either in high school or the first year of college.[35] Although the report suggests that our eminence in basic research is not threatened, relative to Russia, Germany, and other industrialized countries, "our ability to apply technology to our military and industrial pursuits may well be hampered by the relatively low level of scientific and mathematical competence of our nonscientists and, in some respects, by the apparent cooling of science interest among our students generally."[36]

For each of the three R's, literacy standards need to be established to satisfy both parents and teachers.

> The basic skills of reading, writing and computation have to be supplemented by futures skills that better equip students in a race against information production. Thus, we need to teach not only reading, but also speed reading, memory training, listening skills, recall skills, concentration techniques, etc. We need to teach not only writing, but also note-taking, visual-thinking, outlining, precis, abstraction, epigramming, test-taking, and test-design skills. We need to teach not only mathematics, but also budgeting, graphing, statistics, income tax tables, cost-benefits determinations, castastrophe theory, etc.[37]

In addition, the whole range of human knowledge is available for selection of possible curriculum content. What is "absolute must?" What is valuable, though perhaps not essential? What is trivial and wasteful of teaching time?

Just limiting the mission to the maximal development of literacy for all children still leaves schools with a horrendous challenge, a gigantic task. By suggesting literacy development as the basic mission, I do not mean to downgrade the importance of the attitudes, values, self-concepts, multicultural understandings, and behavior patterns that make up the hidden curriculum of school life. The school only shares in education of these matters, however, with the family, the peer group, the church, and other community agencies. It is the literacy function that is and should be the principal school task, though other agencies, expecially the home, will certainly assist in the process.

It is obvious from the Proposition 13 response, the demands for competency testing, and the expressed concerns about the quality of schooling, parents and taxpayers have given notice that they want schools where order and discipline prevail and knowledge and skills are taught. Those students who walk the halls and make no attempt to learn serve only to disrupt the learning of others. Alternative programs must be worked out so they no longer ruin school for everyone else. Parents have also said that they expect teachers to set high though attainable standards, grade rigorously, and correct homework. "The goal of education, traditional or non-traditional, is excellence," exclaims one leading black educator as he endorses the teaching of standard English rather than black English in the public schools. Teaching the latter smacks of educational paternalism.[38]

5. *Teaching Patterns*—Schooling will be quite different in the schools of the future. Not only will there be a great variety to choose from, but the modal pattern will depart from the longstanding tradition of assigning an individual teacher to a class of 25-30 children. Children will be taught in considerably larger and smaller groups, depending on the activity. Instructional teams, not just a series of individual teachers, will staff the school and mini-school units consisting of a head teacher, two to five other senior teachers, some beginning teachers, and a number of paraprofessional and volunteer aides. The overall number of adults to children will probably be somewhat greater, but the number of senior teachers will be down significantly. Teaching teams will develop a more consistent, cohesive, and unified pattern of teaching by careful selection of personnel according to their natural preferences and styles and through systematic daily planning and working together.

Local mini-libraries, materials centers, and tutorial learning locations will be stocked with functional hardware and well-tested, accurately graded software. Instant access to larger software storehouses at the district level will be provided by in-room mini-computers. Considerable learning will occur through computer-assisted instruction, simulation activities, instructional games and toys. Despite the heavier use of instructional equipment, the amount of adult monitoring and interpersonal contact children have will go up as a function of having more people around and more efficiently managed schools. Tutoring by older as well as same-age peers will also become more widely practiced as a way of enhancing the opportunities for human assistance. Overall, student time on learning tasks will increase substantially. Curricular choice will be greater than ever, tempered by regular assessment of student progress on literacy measures.

Rationale: Current research, such as Stallings' work described in Chapter 3, suggests that large group instruction can be a superior means of providing sound literacy instruction. Having a range of human talent and ability available to teach youngsters, rather than a single person, makes possible a much greater range of teaching/grouping patterns. For large group instruction, pupils would have more people to call on for direct teaching and close supervision. Senior citizens, in particular, make excellent volunteers and, like grandparents in the families of a half-century ago, can contribute greatly to the upbringing of the young.

They will offer much in the schools of tomorrow—hearing children read, going over their work, etc. If made genuine partners in teaching teams, they could also become strong political allies and school advocates in the legislative arena.

With appropriate use of volunteers and paid aides, the classroom can become a highly personal interaction and assistance network. The matching of children's natural learning styles with appropriate instructional techniques becomes not just possible but relatively easy to implement with the emerging array of human talent, technological capability, and software resources.

Massive dissemination of great teaching schemes has seldom worked. Successful program implementation requires careful planning and good administrative support at the local level. Perhaps because Bloom's mastery learning model requires such local adaptation, it offers great promise for the improvement of education and, given appropriate implementation, has stepped up the level of learning dramatically in hundreds of classrooms. Commercially prepared instructional materials are increasingly available to help with its adoption.[39] Two enthusiastic proponents state: " . . . most teachers crave systematic, precise pedagogies that show them concrete measurable evidence of student learning."[40]

Bloom's model calls for child-by-child analysis and prescription in order to make the most appropriate assignments in relation to particular cognitive and affective entry characteristics. It is similar in the respect to some programmed instruction models, and studies have consistently shown greater achievement gains and more favorable student attitudes from programmed instruction than from traditional classroom procedures.[41]

Long under development and slow to gain practitioner endorsement, educational technology seems finally on the verge of becoming a useful, effective classroom tool. One expert estimates that almost three million pupils already do some of their schoolwork on computers, double the number four years ago. The relatively low cost of microcomputers and other recent electronic learning aids suggests heavy classroom usage within a few years, if for no other reason than to adopt similar teaching equipment to what middle-class parents will be putting in their homes. Marketing experts estimate that more than 120,000 microcomputers will be sold to schools in 1983 out of one million sales overall.[42] To meet the related software demand, any number of publishing companies are already busy designing a wide range of instructional packages.[43]

So far as effectiveness is concerned, Control Data Corporation advertises that formerly illiterate adults gained the equivalent of one school year in reading from 15 hours on its Plato computer plus 7 hours of outside study, and similar achievement in mathematics from comparable exposure. Research studies indicate that computer-assisted-instruction (CAI), as well as radio and television instruction, is often as effective as conventional procedures and may result in substantial savings of student time.[44] Teaching equipment seems to be particularly useful in the lower grades for drill and practice on mathematics and spelling materials, areas that are often wasteful of student time when done in a group situation.

Regardless of the models being used, the teaching staff, particularly the senior teachers, should be fully conscious of the underlying theory and research base. They must constantly monitor, with research assistance from the central office, its implementation and effectiveness. In short, teaching will not be done willy-nilly with little thought about long-range planning, but with clear theoretical understanding about what one is trying to do and practical plans for how to do it. Whatever the model, teaching procedures need to be carefully thought out and well structured to accomplish their ends. People who conduct the instruction, select the materials, and direct the activities need to know what they are trying to do, be enthusiastic about it, and believe it will work.

I believe that not only Bloom's teaching model but others as well will receive full-scale trial and further development if needed. Teachers need the autonomy yet support of others which only a team effort can provide. They must be willing to change and try out new teaching patterns. Today, they have the vision and desire but usually not the resources and assistance which a small-scale team effort can provide. The loneliness and uncertainty they too often feel can be replaced by excitement over implementing new ideas and seeing child growth as a result.

In a number of recent studies of effective vs. ineffective urban schools, major distinguishing features were found to be the attitudes of the administrative and teaching staff. In schools where poor children learned to read as well as middle-class children, administrators developed a reading program and, either in dictatorial fashion or by close monitoring, saw to it that the plan was fully operational for all children. Generally, there was little difference in types of reading programs or styles of instruction between the two sets of schools. What differed was the insistence on it being fully used on everyone and a belief on the part of teachers that poverty children could learn.

Teachers in "less effective" schools, on the other hand, tended to feel that the home and other non-school factors would make it impossible for them to learn. [45]

6. *Teachers*—The patterns of the future will relieve teachers of the burden of trying to copy a best method of teaching or even of trying to follow supervisory dictates about how to teach. Research shows quite clearly that there is no single method to suit all occasions.

Teachers will generally find the conditions of teaching considerably improved. A team rather than individual teachers will assume overall instructional responsibilities. Even the head teacher will not have the same sense of isolation as present principals. Her responsibilities will be primarily instructional; she will have plenty of assistance in carrying them out.

In gaining greater control over the conditions of teaching, along with higher status and pay opportunity, teachers will lose the obscurity and sense of helplessness that often accompany sole responsibility for a class. No longer will they close the door and do only what they individually choose. What was freedom and autonomy was often loneliness and self doubt as well.

Those days when educators—teachers as well as superintendents—are to be given free reign over the educational system are gone. That is the message behind Proposition 13, the demands for competency testing, the push for tuition tax credit for parents using private schools, the increasing emphasis on cost benefit analysis and other accountability measures. Teachers will be expected to know what they are doing, i.e., state their objectives and explain their procedures, and to be judged on the basis of how well their teaching seems to succeed in the eyes of head teachers and parents particularly. Child accomplishments, or lack of them, will be included in the evaluation criteria.

To achieve higher status and still greater visibility with colleagues and lay people, teachers will have to be more carefully selected and better prepared. We cannot afford to admit and retain the incompetent.

Unlike many professions with strenuous entrance requirements and long years of specialized training and apprenticeship, access to teaching has always been easy and specialized training relatively brief. Within a year or two after graduation from a four-year teacher education program, only a quarter or a third of which is in specialized professional study, a young teacher becomes tenured for life.

Admittedly, some institutions are going to five-year programs, the probationary period for beginning teachers is three years in some states, and inservice teachers are required to go back to school for a course or two every five years to keep their teaching "license" up to date. But these are token improvements. What is really needed, and should occur before 1990, is an integrated sequence of education, specialized training, supervised practice, additional education and experience with increasing responsibility, all within the context of the teaching team instructional system described above. Selection and performance criteria would function at each stage in the sequence to allow only those who are ready for greater responsibilities to proceed. Pay increases would be tied to meritorious performance. Advancement from beginning to senior teacher and eventually head teacher status would be based on increasingly rigorous selection standards.

A plan has been proposed in Virginia for selecting an arbitrarily established number of head teachers in each community and awarding them career teacher certificates. Receiving such a certificate would be analogous to making the all-star team in baseball, achieving "fellow" status in a professional organization, or becoming a full professor in a prestigious university; i.e., it would be highly selective and based on several years of demonstrated top-quality teaching with different types of children, sound knowledge of educational theory and research, and outstanding educational leadership. Selection would be done by a committee of teachers, administrators, and parents. [46]

Salaries of head teachers would approximate those of mid-management businessmen, experienced lawyers and other professionals with above-average incomes. Senior teachers, not heads, would be close behind, well enough paid to insure a career of teaching without financial discomfort. Young and developing teachers, on the other hand, would be paid very modestly so that if they did not demonstrate senior teacher potential relatively early, they could move out of teaching and start new careers without great salary loss.

To keep personnel cost down to realistic limits in order that highly competent teachers could be paid on the scale of present school superintendents and other professionals, one would have to reduce current central office staff and use a higher proportion of paraprofessionals and volunteers. Educational technology should also help to reduce the personnel costs by making teachers more efficient in improving time-on-task. I can envisage a somewhat smaller percentage of the total cost of education going into personnel, but for those teachers who stay and prove to be excellent teachers the financial rewards would be considerably greater.

For all this to happen the present trend toward a takeover of public education by organized labor will have to be stopped, and I predict it will. Teachers' organizations strongly resist the notion of merit pay for teachers. They claim that, because there are few valid and objective ways of assessing teaching performance, pay scales should be based solely on academic credentials, years of experience, and other objective measures. [47] They claim that wherever merit-pay schemes have been tried they have only caused dissention, low morale and complaints about administrative favoritism. "Teachers," they say, "are supposed to cooperate, not compete."

The public, by and large, feels quite the opposite. Parents and non-educators alike know that some teachers are better than others. They do not buy the idea that you cannot distinguish between them. It is done all the time in business and industry. Why, then, is education so different?

The argument is stirring increased debate and positions may soon be altered. Wanting to raise standards, even former Secretary of Education Shirley M. Hufstedler tried to find concrete ways to "pay public tribute to teachers who display unique talent in the classroom."[48] In a delightful article entitled, "Would Bear Bryant Teach In the Public Schools? The Need for Teacher Incentives," a social studies teacher argues forcefully for a merit-pay system to attract and keep those who strive to excel as teachers. Among other well-articulated points, he states: "Teachers soon discover that being an excellent teacher is tremendously demanding, while being mediocre is extremely easy."[49]

The essence of these concerns is the present lack of an incentive system. Without some means of being recognized in significant, tangible ways for excellence of performance, many potentially great teachers are not going to consider a life-time career in education under today's highly frustrating teaching conditions. Without some hope of greater long-term benefits, the sacrifices in time, salary, and psychic energy are no longer justified. There is no career ladder whatsoever for the person who wants to remain a teacher rather than become an administrator. As one teacher told me just before quitting her position for one in real estate: "There's no future or place to go once you hit the classroom if you are at all competitive."

Despite teacher organization resistance and even acknowledging that there are more than two million members of either the NEA or AFT, I still believe a merit system of some sort can and must be installed. If it takes power politics to accomplish it, the PTA membership of six million could be solicited along with millions of others. But confrontation, hopefully, will not be necessary.

The silent majority of American teachers, which entered the field partly for altruistic reasons, has always emulated the professional model of doing what is needed regardless of pay, schedule, or resource limitations. Because their altruistic nature has been taken advantage of too often, teachers finally responded to calls for organized effort to protect their rights. Underneath, however, they are still service-motivated professionals, and when new opportunities arise for them to function and be treated like professionals under the proposed 1990 system, they will respond accordingly.

In their emerging roles as true professionals, they will have to demonstrate a range and depth of competencies not now required of teachers. They, not just superintendents and college professors, will become articulate spokesmen for education. They will open their schools to close public scrutiny by way of showing test scores, learning curves, and instructional plans, and by involving parents in curriculum decisions and even program operations. There will be no place for inarticulate, overly shy, poorly educated, or generally ineffective teachers.

As instructional leaders, head teachers will need to be more conversant with educational theory and its relationship with practice than others on their teams or than well-educated community leaders. They will need to know educational research, what it can tell and what it cannot tell. They will have to be receptive to change when good research indicates change is needed. They will tend to react less defensively to negative evaluations or legitimate criticisms. They will be "under the gun," and they must be ready to try new procedures when old ones fail to work.

Head teachers must be broadly educated, widely read, and interested in ideas. They must also be self-assured and socially adept, able to interact comfortably and impressively with a wide range of people. There will be no place for the social isolate who cannot work effectively with others on the team.

Above all, they must be top-notch teachers of children. They must be able to control children well and instill an interest in learning. They must demonstrate genuine affection for children, a real concern for their welfare, and great enthusiasm for teaching.

Those who become head teachers must also demonstrate good management skills, because they will be responsible for directing a show with a cast of over a hundred. They must not become wedded to their administrative tasks either, as their primary function will be making the *instructional* show run smoothly.

They will be complete professionals in role, competency, pay and respect. Those who make it will deserve it. Those who do not will leave the field.

Rationale:

> Teaching . . . is honored and disdained, praised as "dedicated service" and lampooned as "easy work." It is permeated with the rhetoric of professionalism, yet features incomes below those earned by workers with considerably less education. It is middle-class work in which more and more participants use bargaining strategies developed by wage-earners in factories.[50]

In recent years the second pole of these dichotomies has been receiving the attention. It is time to make the first predominant. And instead of reasserting the "rhetoric of professionalism," we need to impose the condition itself. We do this by changing the role, the status, the training, and the salary level of teachers. We make it considerably more selective by increasing the applicant pool through offering the promise of a better career. Where most men currently in teaching tend to be transient, soon to move into administration or leave the field, we instill the possibiliity of full career opportunities as teachers with sufficient pay to support a family comfortably. For women, already the more permanent segment in teaching, we offer at least as challenging an occupation as those which are opening up in business and industry.

The recent oversupply of teachers makes the early 1980s an opportune time to tighten up on access to the field. It also provides a good chance to instill recognition of teaching competence as the principal basis for salary improvement and advancement in the system.

With its lockstep salary schedules and easy tenure features, public education is a century-old monopoly that has grown lazy and inefficient. It needs a competitive element which will offer those who wish to strive hard and demonstrate superior accomplishment the opportunity to do so.

I have seen many young, effective teachers, three or four years out of college, become disenchanted with teaching because, unless they want to become an administrator, "there's no place to go." While we may not need the hard-driving, aggressive business or sales persons of the what-makes-Sammy-run-variety, education should attract mature, poised, intelligent, and personable people equal to the best in any other field. It needs people who not only want to work with young people, be of service to humanity, and make a difference in the world by what they do, but also who want to grow and develop themselves and have a career that rewards them for doing so.

To establish this sense of professionalism and to find the means to pay senior and head teachers appropriately, we must restructure the teaching staff. Instead of all teachers—young and old, experienced and inexperienced—doing the same thing and getting very close to the same salaries, we differentiate responsibilities and spread out pay differentials. We also draw on relatively low paid paraprofessionals and volunteers who under proper direction can become strong, useful team members.

We also step up the use of computer-assisted-instruction and other technology, which under reasonable supervision can provide good instructional help. It cannot do the job by itself because the human component is so vital to the teaching process. But education is one of the few fields of work where labor-saving devices have yet to be put to work. Even with such devices, teaching, when it is done right, demands hard work and long hours.

7.   *Finances and Feds*—Federal and state support for the operation of local schools will be up, both in dollars and on a percentage basis. Despite such increases, however, a slightly smaller percentage of the GNP may well go into education as the increasing political strength of senior citizens brings about greater health and social security benefits.

Overall, the federal government will contribute 15 percent, the state government 60 percent and local tax resources 25 percent of all school expenditures (currently 8, 44, and 48 respectively).[51] Almost all of the federal contributions and the majority of state support will be by bloc grants or formula funding tied to population statistics with equalizing formulas to make up for differences in communities' capacities to finance schools. Local authorities will be in almost complete control of how money is to be spent. The only substantial sum of federal money that will not be passed on directly to local districts will be used for basic and applied research on the status and processes of education. Similarly, most state money will be passed on to localities with some held back for state research efforts and technical assistance.

Rationale: Recent cutbacks in financial resources have been devastating, especially to urban school systems. Programs have been eliminated, and classroom aides, bus attendants, librarians, home economics, physical education, driver education, art, music, and other specialized teachers let go. In budget-balancing efforts, for example, the

Newark Board of Education dismissed almost one-quarter of its employees in December, 1978, and Washington, D.C. cut out over a thousand positions in August, 1980.[52]

Education is one of our largest labor-intensive industries, and as such its costs have risen much faster during a highly inflationary period than those of capital-intensive industries.[53] As a result, two major changes are likely in the conduct and financing of public education.

First will be efforts to improve the efficiency of instructional delivery by increasing the use of educational technology and the employment of low-cost aides and volunteers. Past efforts to use technology failed because, at the time, there was no incentive to put it to work and because it had not yet reached a sufficiently advanced state of perfected hardware and software to demonstrate its utility. Today neither constraint holds. The technology has become available at low enough cost to be purchased privately by middle-class parents, and other institutions (i.e., business, industry) are ready to put it to work if schools do not. Costs of machines and accompanying software are no longer prohibitive. Machines seem capable, furthermore, of delivering some aspects of instruction, i.e., tutoring, routine practice, and problem simulation, at least as well as traditional teaching procedures.[54] If public schools do not begin to adopt them, alternative institutions will, and at lower costs. Such a trend would further undermine public support for common schools and stimulate additional development of voucher systems and competing institutions. The United States has attempted to educate at public expense a much larger segment of the population for a longer period of time than any other major country. Unless our schools find ways of cutting costs in the delivery of instruction, our willingness to continue this obligation could easily erode.

Secondly, major changes are likely in the sources of funding. Trends already underway in the seventies will bring about an improved, balanced and more adequate overall support during the eighties. Federal support will increase, proportionate to local taxes, because it has the larger source of supply, and the cost of education long ago outgrew what local property taxes could provide. In addition, court decisions (e.g., Serrano vs. Priest) necessitate equalizing educational efforts across communities regardless of the wealth underlying a school district. For similar reasons, state efforts will be increased, proportionate to local financing.

A critical issue in these funding shifts is what implications they pose for the control of education. Where will the power be vested for making the critical decisions needed to operate the schools? Is it possible for funding to come from one source and control from another?

Not only is it possible, but for a number of reasons I think it is likely. The citizenry seems genuinely ready to do away with highly centralized, bureaucratic solutions to our various problems. People are generally disgruntled over heavy-handed, complicated government directives. What started as simple services for addressing well-established needs gradually turned into highly complex bureaucratic agencies whose operations are conducted via an unintelligible mass of legalistic regulations and endless reporting directives. There is widespread disenchantment over government operations being directed and conducted from afar.

In addition, the Constitution itself leaves the primary responsibility to the states, and states traditionally, through distribution of general aid on a per pupil basis, have tended to give much of the control to local school boards. These traditions run deep. Indeed, much of the complaint about education today is over the dictates that come from Richmond, Washington or the courts. Leading educators in Washington have been careful to keep the various Department of Education units from prescribing particular courses or tests lest a national curriculum might be implied. Even in Richmond, mandated competency test batteries represent a mixture of state and local packaging.

Complaints about federal and state directives, and the mass of regulations and reports they necessitate, have reached sympathetic ears in Congress and the various legislatures. One state superintendent testified that federal programs were responsible for 84 percent of his state's data burden; yet only 7 percent of the state's total funds for education came from federal sources.[55] Even though the feds contribute only a small percentage of the total support of education, their clout has seemed much more because of the way money has been given out.

Strong sentiment now exists for reducing that clout. The public increasingly recognizes that our teachers and administrators are being stifled by regulations and paperwork emanating from categorical funding and court decisions. The only hope for improving the system is simplifying the demands as much as possible and allowing greater discretion for meeting them at the local level.

Just a sampling of extra legal obligations that educators assume today that did not exist two decades ago shows how much the freedom to manage classes and schools has been cut back:

I. Q. tests cannot be used for placing children in special education classes—(Peckman decision applicable in Northern California).[56]

Search procedures for drugs on children's clothes or in their lockers must not violate their rights of privacy.[57]

Teachers must report children they suspect to be victims of child abuse without violating parents' privacy rights.[58]

P.L. 94-142 regulations stipulate that a handicapped child cannot be deprived of receiving his educational program for more than two days, thus limiting a possible disciplinary suspension to that period.

Since the Wood vs. Strickland case in 1975 upheld the rights of students accused of troublemaking to due-process treatment, the number of students expelled from school has decreased by 30 percent.[59]

Extra funds to meet many of these added burdens, furthermore, have not been provided. PL 94-142, for example, mandates an appropriate program, regardless of cost; yet many local school districts received less than $200 supplemental funding per handicapped child in 1980 to meet this obligation. When extra costs come out of existing funds, as they often do, they serve also to decrease the program for non-handicapped students.

Local school districts constantly struggle to meet the demands of their local constituencies, but they are also forced to overcome obstacles placed in their paths by their friends in the state and federal education bureaucracies who tend to strangle the local district through a multiplicity of regulations. Accountability comes down more to suspicion and distrust than to mutual effort toward the solution of serious problems.[60]

Because of increasingly widespread recognition that "top-down directives" typically accompany categorical funding, one major change I expect will be toward increased funding by bloc grants or simple formula funding on a head-count basis. Prominent politicians in the new Republican administration have consistently endorsed such a notion. Equalizing formulas can be used to provide extra funding for urban or low-income districts; but, overall, federal and even state funds can be distributed relatively simply to localities as general aid with local authorities having considerable discretion in their use.

With most money going directly to school districts on a per-pupil basis, the present stifling hand of central government control could be eased. Accountability would go directly to local governing groups where school mission and curriculum variations reflective of varying community mores and expectations could be taken into account.

A strong push for bloc-grant funding, i.e., general aid, has been made in Congress during the past decade. One result has been to keep the federal education bureaucracy from growing but to increase instead the size and responsibility of state education departments in order to direct and monitor categorical funds. Approximately half the staff positions in such departments are supported by federal funds. But because the funding is still categorical, complex directives covering regulations of the type cited in Chapter 2 have to be distributed and compliance reports collected in return. In the groundswell of opposition toward such regulations and particularly in response to the conservative posture of the American voting public in the 1980 election, bloc grant funding will become increasingly popular. The biggest obstacle to this happening is the popularity among politicians of categorical grants for specific educational programs rather than general aid. They like to be able to say what they did on the people's behalf, such as sponsoring a bill for "the gifted."

One other reason why general aid will gradually replace categorical grants is that, no matter how carefully written the regulations, federal bureaucrats are too few and too far away to cover the 16,000 school districts in existence; neither do state education departments have sufficient personnel to direct and monitor what should go on closely enough to do it well. We shall have to trust local school authorities to run the schools, give them the resources, and remove the constraints if the problems of public education are to be corrected.

Because these constraints are imposed by central government regulators, the most effective means currently available to an individual parent for expressing a complaint about the system is to contact congressmen or legislators and hope for some correction of the long-term situation. The process is much too tedious, and to correct a situation that might help one's child, it is virtually hopeless.

Let me add something about the federal research effort. This is the one area, other than collecting and distributing tax revenues without strings attached, where the federal government has a legitimate function and one that is badly needed. I have mentioned the weak research base which underlies our present educational system. There are very few important questions educators can ask where good research-supported answers can be given.

After searching in vain for solid, consistent research findings to help answer such politically important questions as what is the relationship of pupil achievement and class size, teaching experience, and the amount of education teachers have, or the level of expenditures and school performance, one Congressman (Stavisky of New York) made a strong plea for improved federal efforts to strengthen the research base for education, especially as it relates to policy questions.[61] State and local policy-makers also need the kind of research information that federal government agencies are in the best position to obtain. Because of heavy competition from direct program costs, local and even state school budgets are usually very limited in the amount of research money they provide.

Not only is there a general need for more research, but recent improvements in research technology and design now make sound, useful studies on policy-relevant questions possible, despite the complexity of the educational enterprise. A number of studies have been cited in this volume which provide solid information about how well schooling is going and why. Almost all of them were specially sponsored research, i.e., supported by outside foundations or competitive federal government grants.

In the future research will be stepped up a thousand-fold. It will be stimulated by two needs: (a) to obtain sufficient descriptive information about what is going on in local schools to satisfy local citizen expectations, and (b) to provide political leaders with the information they need about the condition of education. In both respects the federal education agency will have a legitimate and necessary role. For money to be available to local school districts for evaluation and research purposes I would even propose categorical aid toward that end.

It is clear that, for the first of these functions, local administrators must hire good evaluation and research personnel. Instructional leadership will pass from the present central staff directly to head teachers, and curriculum development and instructional programming will become the responsibility of teaching teams. The main function of the central administration, therefore, will be helping teams get the resources to do the job. This will include providing research expertise and assistance to gather the kinds of data about children, instruction, and learning needed to operate programs, assess their effectiveness, and provide empirical information for their improvement.

For the second of these functions, politicians must be assured, as with the medical field, that progress is being made on a basic societal problem; namely, providing the most enlightened, literate citizenry in the world. In our country, as in any democracy, one of the greatest fears is that government will gain control over the thoughts and minds of the citizenry. There is great concern that the current testing movement could lead eventually to the adoption of the same standardized test battery for all states and localities, so as to permit the best comparisons to be made between school systems. There is also great fear of any national curriculum effort. It is politically unacceptable, therefore, to allow the federal government a greater hand in these areas.

What is needed from Washington instead is a much greater research effort, which school systems are not capable of mounting on their own. Almost all the empirical information we now have about the educative process has come from outside funding, which typically costs much more than local school budgets permit.

The feds should get out of the massive program development arena and the sponsorship of Title I, bilingual education, community education, personnel preparation, staff development, and all the other special brainchildren of the current politicos. Disseminating fully packaged cure-alls from on high has not worked and will not in the future. What is needed instead is much more sound research about teaching and learning, from which local teaching staffs can draw ideas and strengthen their theoretical bases for designing and testing out their own programs.

Carefully designed research of promising local school programs is needed to determine their quality and analyze the critical teaching-learning components in order to build empirically supported theories of education. Even the effectiveness of alternative schools cannot be well documented at the moment because the quality of research conducted on such programs is so weak.[62]

The budget of NIE and the other educational research units in the new Department of Education ought to be multiplied many times. Although a research bureaucracy on the scale of NIH's may not be justifiable, considerably more educational research effort would be possible if some of the non-productive federal programs were eliminated.

Credibility Restored

The decade of the seventies brought increased criticism of the American school system. Dropping SAT scores, illiterate teachers, school vandalism, and pupil drug abuse were among topics of complaint making headlines in popular periodicals and becoming subjects of regular television coverage. The charges were great and the answers typically less than reassuring that all is well with the public schools. Confidence about the way schools are being run has slipped sufficiently to threaten their continued existence. Our longstanding support of free, common, compulsory, universal schooling for all youngsters through high school may be nearing an end.

In this volume, I have attempted not only to analyze these criticisms and assess their validity but to focus more broadly on the current state of public education so as to attain perspective on where it might be heading. While there is always value in developing foresight out of carefully achieved hindsight, it seems especially important to do so now when so many underlying educational issues need resolution. Struggles over mission, control, financing, staffing, and schooling itself have never been so great.

Without attempting to digest again the major criticisms and my assessment of their validity, let me highlight just a few of the well-documented accomplishments of public school systems up to now:

1. While some test scores have declined, others have advanced over the past several decades. Compared to similar students in other Western nations, our top students are second to none in the all-important skill of reading comprehension; they rank high also in several other areas. For all youngsters, reading achievement scores are somewhat higher today than for similar-age children in the 1940s. (See pp. 7-17, 116-117 for more details of these and other findings.) Although some youngsters have been going through high school without learning to read, write, or calculate at minimum levels, overall test results based on all the population age-wise suggest the schools are probably teaching the basic skills better than ever before and better than schools in most other countries.

2. We have made a considerably greater effort to teach all children for a longer period of time than any other major country. Whereas only about 6 percent of all youths finished high school in 1900, about 80 percent do today and half of them go on to college.

3. During the past several decades we have done away with a legally supported, racially defined, dual system of schools. Whereas only one in four black children completed high school in 1950, three of four do today. As one columnist expressed this accomplishment:

In 30 years, the public schools were opened to a huge underclass of young people. Will anyone argue that this generation, now completing high school, is behind those children who, a generation ago, quit in the 7th or 8th grade?[63]

In short, no other education system in the world opens so many doors to an improved way of life.

4. Education does make a difference and a big one—in earning power and a higher standard of living, in knowledge and even the ability to learn, and in the socialization of the young into the larger society. Furthermore, not all of the recent experiments with educational programming have failed. Although almost no federal programs have been effectively and broadly disseminated, many innovations have been successful where the expertise and resources were sufficient to permit good implementation. In brief, the R and D efforts of recent years are paying off.

We tend to forget these magnificent accomplishments and fail to recognize that they have cost less than what baby-sitters alone would charge. With all this success, why then all the complaints and loss of confidence in the educational establishment? Probably for several reasons.

One is a weak public relations effort. Things that go wrong tend to make news; things that go as expected do not. Educators must find ways to display and even dramatize their accomplishments in public. They need also to speak out boldly against unwarranted criticism and refute questionable charges. Schools are under the spotlight as never before, and they need articulate leadership to explain all that is going on.

A second reason for loss of public confidence is the increasing confusion over mission. Different groups expect different accomplishments from the schools. Business leaders want schools to provide job entry skills and an appreciation of the free-enterprise system. Middle-class parents are concerned most about how well their youngsters will be prepared for college. Low-income families see the schools as providers of nutritional and health benefits. Minorities expect equal access to educational opportunities even if it means special treatment to remedy deficiencies. The same is true with parents of the handicapped. Women expect comparable athletic programs with men and removal of sex-biased curricula. Church groups clamor for recognition of their own religious holidays. Lawyers and politicians are insistent that schools be conducted in a manner that protects such rights as privacy and due process for children and their families.

Never before has so much been expected of one institution. The traditional mission of schools fifty years ago was much more narrowly focused than that of today, in part, because social norms were more clearly established and understood. The shifting mix of today's diverse social norms accounts for much of the confusion over school goals. There are just too many people with different expectations for the schools to meet all of them.

A third reason is the public's disillusionment with most of its institutions, i.e., government bureaucracies, big business, organized labor, the professions. By comparison the schools do not fare too badly. A recent survey by the Education Commission of the States found a higher percentage of people recommending increased funds for public schools than for any of several other government services such as recreation, health and hospitals, sanitation, police and fire departments.[64]

In another survey of public confidence in the people running institutions in business, television and the press, religion, education, the military, Congress, the Supreme Court, and several other areas, education ranked third behind medicine and the scientific community. Ratings, furthermore, dropped substantially in all areas between 1973 and 1978, not just in education.[65]

At least one other reason is the lack of consensus among teachers and other educators over teaching goals and methods, curricula, grading patterns, class management practices and other instructional concerns. While differences between one teacher or school and another have always existed in such matters, the heavy publicity given curricular reform following the Sputnik launching and Lyndon Johnson's promise of a great society through improved education gave visibility and hope to specific programs; it assigned to a non-unified educational establishment the burden of bringing about major social change. Now that the presumed virtues of "open education," the "new math," and other innovations of the sixties have turned out to be dismal failures, educators who pioneered these efforts have lost their credibility and clout. Hopefully, as education's knowledge base continues to be strengthened as a function of increasing research, educators will achieve greater agreement over what constitutes good and bad practice. As they do, their credibility with the public should return.

Although confidence in our public schools has dropped, it is still far from destroyed. Surveys tend to show greater satisfaction from parents who have children in the school than from non-parents or those whose children are not in school.[66] As the proportion of adults with children in school decreases in the years ahead, necessary support for education will have to be generated from those without school-age children if the system is not to fail.

It is imporant, therefore, to address the many complaints positively and convincingly at several different levels. A suburban parent takes her child out of the local public school saying, "The teachers are spending all their time with the kids who are acting up." That school's principal must find out whether such a charge is true and if so, correct the situation; if not, talk with parents about the false rumor.

When well-known, influential people like author James Michener and presidential adviser Amitai Etzioni openly criticize the schools in the media, strong, articulate voices must be raised in response. When the former suggests that youngsters who cannot be disciplined in school and merely disrupt learning opportunities for others be allowed to leave school at age 14,[67] he should be questioned about who then assumes responsibility for these early dropouts and what are the likely consequences for both them and society. With Etzioni, the complaint is over mission and sending an absurd number of young adults to college. "In reindustrializing America, there will be more demand for less-skilled labor and less demand for highly professional people. We will need more coal miners, not more graduate students."[68]

One must take issue with his underlying assumption that the purpose of education is solely job preparation. Arguments over the appropriate mission for American public schools must take place at the highest levels and by people responsive to a broad electorate. As the mission of public education achieves clarity, at least some of the voices of complaint can then be stilled. Mission clarification is particularly needed among members of Congress and legislatures, where much of the pressure for the schools to assume their present, diverse, and confused burdens originated. The schools are being asked to do far too much to do anything well. It will require strong professional leadership and considerable public debate to establish needed priorities. Also essential is responsible, aggressive political activity to remove the regulatory trivia and change the funding patterns so that the control of education can go back to the local level where it belongs.

Accountability may be mandated but it cannot be monitored out of Sacramento or Washington except in very general terms. The distances are too great, the resources too few, and the cost too high. Quality education, where it is missing, can only be restored by demanding it at the local level, obtaining the resources, having the discretion to prescribe how they are to be used, and holding specific individuals accountable for bringing it about.

With local school boards, school-site councils, and other citizen groups much more in control, professional educators would have little excuse but to deliver what it is possible to deliver. They would need to be armed with good information about how well the schools are doing in reaching community-developed literacy objectives. The public should expect much better data regarding how well each child is doing compared with other youngsters his age elsewhere, how much learning occurs in each of the schools and mini-schools, how time is really spent in each school including actual time-on-task research data, and what is actually being taught. Administrators and head teachers must be expected to explain fully and accurately what goes on and how well it is working. If after a reasonable period serious deficiencies are not corrected to parent's satisfaction, personnel changes should be made. Fair and reasonable accountability demands can be satisfied in direct, face-to-face interaction to a much greater extent than our present system of statewide competency exams, burdensome reports to government agencies, and heavy-handed regulatory demands from on high will ever permit.

One of my greatest beliefs is that the public will continue to support a system of universal public education on at least its present scale if its quality can be improved and credibility restored. Whether or not this will happen depends on making politicians accountable for better financing plans rather than buying votes with categorical programs, returning the control of education to local authorities, and holding teachers and administrators responsible for developing sound programs of instruction to match the desires of local citizenries. While the public wants some choice, and programs designed to meet the needs of all children require it, parents and citizens generally also want clear evidence that children are learning.

The public at this time is asking for improved quality of teaching and learning. To the extent that clear evidence indicates that this happens in community after community, complaints will disappear and pride will be restored in what has to be the greatest educational experiment ever attempted, the American public school system.

NOTES AND REFERENCES

Chapter One

1. Charles M. Frye, *Newsweek,* September 3, 1979, p. 13.

2. Mary A. Golladay and Jay Noell (eds), *The Condition of Education,* 1978 Edition, Statistical Report (Washington: National Center for Education Statistics), p. 173.

3. "Literacy among Youths 12-17 Years," *The National Health Survey,* Series II, No. 131 (Washington: U.S. Office of Education, December 1973), p. 15.

4. Harold L. Hodgkinson, "Education Does Make a Difference," *Educational Leadership,* 35, December 1977, pp. 222-225.

5. Harold Howe, II, "Tests and Schooling," presentation at the National Conference on Achievement Testing (Washington, March 1-3, 1978).

6. Unless otherwise indicated, the test findings reported in this section appear in one or both of the following documents: Report of the Advisory Panel on the Scholastic Aptitude Test Score Decline (Willard Wirtz, chairman), *On Further Examination* (New York: College Entrance Examination Board, 1977); Evelyn Stern Silver (ed.), *Declining Test Scores,* a conference report (Washington: National Institute of Education, February 1976).

7. Phillip R. Rever and Lawrence K. Kojaku, "Access, Attrition, Test Scores and Grades of College Entrants and Persisters: 1965-1973," presentation at the American Association of Collegiate Registrars and Admissions Officers National Conference, Minneapolis, Minnesota, April, 1975 (available through The American College Testing Program, Iowa City, Iowa 52240).

8. Stanley Ahmann, "How Much Are Young People Learning?" in Arthur J. Newman (ed.), *In Defense of the American Public School* (Cambridge, Mass.: Schenkman Publishing, 1978), pp. 82-83.

9. George Neill, "Washington Report," *Phi Delta Kappan,* 61, November 1979, p. 157.

10. Annegret Harnischfeger and David E. Wiley, "The Marrow of Achievement Test Score Declines," *Educational Technology,* 16, June 1976, pp. 5-14.

11. Ibid.

12. Leo A. Munday, "Changing Test Scores, Especially Since 1970," *Phi Delta Kappan,* 60, March 1979, pp. 496-499.

13. Arthur I. Gates, *Reading Attainment in Elementary Schools: 1957 and 1937* (New York: Teachers College, Columbia University, 1961).

14. John C. Flanagan, "Changes in School Levels of Achievement: Project TALENT Ten and Fifteen Year Retests," *Educational Researcher,* 5, September 1976, pp. 9-12.

15. Christopher Jencks, "The Wrong Answer for Schools Is: (b) Back to the Basics," *Washington Post,* February 19, 1978, pp. C1, 4, 5.

16. Ibid.

17. Golladay and Noell, *Condition of Education,* Table 2.23.

18. Munday, "Changing Test Scores," pp. 496-499.

19. See reference 3; Also, Ralph W. Tyler, quoted in Ron Brandt, "Conflicting Views on Competency Testing in Florida," *Educational Leadership,* 36, November 1978, p. 101.

20. Roger Farr, Leo Fay, and Harold H. Negley, *Then and Now: Reading Achievement in Indiana,* 1944-45 and 1976 (Bloomington, Ind.: School of Education, Indiana University, 1978).

21. *U.S. News & World Report,* July 25, 1977, p. 75.

22. This comparison is based on the not unreasonable assumption that the 20% who completed high school in 1923 were the academic elite of their age-group.

23. "Student attitudes and discipline," was the most frequently cited hindrance among secondary school teachers to their rendering their best possible service, Golladay and Noell, *Condition of Education,* p. 54.

24. Barbara Tuchman, *Forbes,* March 5, 1979, p. 26.

25. George H. Gallup, *The Gallup Poll: Public Opinion 1972-1977* (Wilmington, Del.: Scholarly Resources, 1978), p. 494 cites the median response.

26. William M. Bocks, "Non-Promotion: A Year to Grow?" *Educational Leadership,* 34, February 1977, pp. 379-383.

27. Sam Taylor, quoted in Pat Lewis, "High School Today: Discipline," *Washington Star,* January 1, 1980, p. C2.

28. Thelma Johnson, "A Parting Shot from a Teacher," *New York Times,* June 23, 1979.

29. Stanley M. Elam (ed.), *A Decade of Gallup Polls of Attitudes Toward Education* (Bloomington, Ind.: Phi Delta Kappa, 1978), p. 341.

30. *Violent Schools—Safe Schools,* The Safe School Study Report to the Congress, Executive Summary (Washington: National Institute of Education, February 1978).

31. Golladay and Noell, *Condition of Education,* p. 264.

32. David L. Manning, "Inflation, Education and the After-School Job," *Wall Street Journal,* March 11, 1980.

33. Whatever pay improvements occurred between 1950 and 1975 have eroded since then. Between June 1978 and June 1979 schoolteachers lost more in "real pay," i.e., after allowing for inflation and taxes, than most other categories of workers. See *U.S. News & World Report,* October 1, 1979, p. 53.

34. Nancy B. Dearman and Valena White Plisko, *The Condition of Education,* 1979 Edition, Statistical Report (Washington: National Center for Education Statistics), p. 82.

35. Donald M. Medley, *Teacher Competence and Teacher Effectiveness, A Review of Process—Product Research* (Washington: American Association of Colleges for Teacher Education, August 1977).

36. Christopher Jencks et al., *Inequality: A Reassessment of the Effect of Family and Schooling in America* (New York: Basic Books, 1972); James S. Coleman et al., *Equality of Educational Opportunity* (Washington: Government Printing Office, 1966). Reexamination of the Coleman survey indicates that it was not designed to permit

conclusions about either what goes on in schools or how it contributes to student achievement, rather to determine the extent schools achieve equality of opportunity and the relation of various resources to that accomplishment. Interpreting the findings of the Coleman report as evidence that schools have little effect on student learning is a gross misrepresentation of what it does say. See George F. Madaus, Peter W. Airasian, and Thomas Kellaghan, *School Effectiveness: A Reassessment of the Evidence* (New York: McGraw-Hill, 1980), pp. 175-190.

37. Quoted in *U.S. News & World Report,* September 11, 1978, p. 51.

38. At least 7% of a national sample of teachers cited each of these factors in response to being asked what hindered them most in rendering their best possbile service. See Golladay and Noell, *Condition of Education,* p. 54.

39. Harry S. Broudy, "The Fiduciary Basis of Education: A Crisis in Credibility," *Phi Delta Kappan,* 59, October 1977, pp. 87-90.

40. Because of school dropouts during high school, it is difficult to find representative achievement test norms for 18-year-olds. Norm tables typically indicate, however, that 5-10% of beginning ninth-graders would score below the sixth-grade mean. See, for example, the Advanced battery Norms Booklet, Form A, Stanford Achievement Test for Reading (New York: Harcourt Brace Jovanovich, 1973).

41. Estimates from the Virginia State Department of Education.

42. Henry M. Brickell, "Seven Key Notes on Minimal Competency Testing," *Educational Leadership,* 35, April 1978, p. 554.

43. Judith T. Evans, "An Activity Analysis of U.S. Traditional, U.S. Open, British Open Classrooms," in Bernard Spodek and Herbert J. Walberg (eds.), *Studies in Open Education* (New York: Agathon Press, 1975), pp. 155-168.

44. Michael Novak, Jeane Kirkpatrick, and Anne Crutcher, *Values in an American Government Textbook, Three Appraisals* (Washington: Georgetown University, 1978).

45. *U. S. News & World Report,* June 4, 1979, p. 51.

46. From a speech by J.W. Marriott, Jr., appearing under the heading, "This Is Education?" *Forbes,* June 12, 1978, p. 24.

47. Benjamin S. Bloom, *Stability and Change in Human Characteristics* (New York: John Wiley, 1964). A consortium of longitudinal studies provides recent evidence that children who participate in preschool programs are less likely to be assigned to a special class or retained in grade as they go through school than comparable children without preschool experience. See Dearman and Plisko, *Condition of Education,* 1980, p. 197.

48. Frank E. Armbruster, "The More We Spend, the Less Children Learn," *New York Times Magazine,* August 28, 1977, pp. 9-11, 53-60.

49. Ibid.

50. *Evaluating Compensatory Education,* An Interim Report on the NIE Compensatory Education Study (Washington: National Institute of Education, December 30, 1976).

51. NEA Research Memo, *Financial Status of the Public Schools,* 1979 (Washington: National Education Association, 1979), p. 46.

52. *The Compensatory Education Study: Executive Summary* (Washington: National Institute of Education, July 1978), p. 7; The National Advisory Council on the Education of Disadvantaged Children, U.S. Education Department, *The Office of Education Administers Changes in a Law: Agency Response to Title I, ESEA Amendments of 1978* (NTS: Research Corporation, May 1980), p. 9.

53. Robert Rossi, "Summaries of Major Title I Evaluations, 1966-1977," prepared for the National Institute of education, DHEW, July 1977, ED 145-012; as cited in Karen Hill-Scott and J. Eugene Grigsby, "Some policy recommendations for compensatory education," *Phi Delta Kappan,* 60, February 1979, p. 444.

54. Donald A. Trismen, Michael I. Waller, and Gita Wilder, *A Descriptive and Analytic Study of Compensatory Reading Programs,* Final Report, Volume I (Washington: U.S. Department of Health, Education and Welfare, Office of Education, Office of Planning, Budgeting, and Evaluation, December 1975).

55. Thomas C. Thomas and Sol. H. Pelavin, *Patterns in ESEA Title I Reading Achievement* (Menlo Park, Calif.: Stanford Research Institute, March 1976).

56. Ibid., p. 37.

57. *The Effects of Student Services on Student Development* (Washington: National Institute of Education, September 30, 1977), p. 19.

58. NIE Compensatory Education Study, Collected Reports, Vol. 7, Chapter 4, "The Instructional Dimensions Follow-up," 1978, pp. 273-279.

59. *Effects of Student Services,* p. 24.

60. Launor F. Carter, Educational Effectiveness: Some Results from the Sustaining Effects Study (Santa Monica, Calif.: System Development Corp., September 1979) (Typewritten drafts.)

61. *Report on Education Research* (Washington: Capitol Publications, February 21, 1979), p. 5.

62. Malcolm N. Danoff, *Evaluation of the Impact of ESEA Title VII Spanish-English Bilingual Education Program,* Overview of Study and Findings (Palo Alto, Calif.: American Institutes for Research, March 1978).

63. "Value of Integration Is Illusory, says Coleman," *Phi Delta Kappan,* 60, November 1978, p. 156.

64. "Forced Busing Does Cause White Flight, Say Rand Researchers after Six-Year Study," *Phi Delta Kappan,* 60, November 1978, p. 156.

65. *News Exchange* (Washington: Association for Supervision and Curriculum Development, December 1978).

66. Paul Berman and Milbrey Wallin McLaughlin, *Federal Programs Supporting Educational Change,* vol. VIII, Implementing and Sustaining Innovations (Santa Monica, Calif.: Rand Corp., May 1978).

67. Harvey J. Brudner, "Gedanken Experiments in Educational Cost Effectiveness," *The Journal,* March/April 1977, p. 33.

68. Although class size research has been interpreted as showing "that few pupil benefits can be expected from reducing class size if teachers continue to use the same teaching techniques that they used in larger classes" [see Educational Research Service, *Class Size: A Summary of Research* (Arlington, Va.: ERS, 1978, p. 69)],

meta-analyses of such research do indicate that class size and children's achievement are inversely correlated, i.e., achievement tends to go up as class size goes down. The relationship is not particularly strong, however, until class sizes are reduced below 20. See Gene V. Glass and Mary Lee Smith, "Meta-Analyses of Research on the Relationship of Class-Size and Achievement," *Evaluation and Policy Analysis,* January/February 1979, pp. 2-16. See also Mary Lee Smith and Gene V. Glass, *Relationship of Class-Size to Classroom Processes, Teacher Satisfaction and Pupil Affect: A Meta-Analysis* (San Francisco: Far West Laboratory for Educational Research and Development, July 1979).

69. Theodore H. Martland, "Costly Schools That Do Not Educate," *Business Week,* January 30, 1978, p. 9.

70. Interview with Paul Gann, "We Intend to Stay Involved," *U.S. News & World Report,* June 26, 1978, p. 20.

71. Mary A. Golladay, *The Condition of Education,* 1976 Edition (Washington: National Center for Education Statistics, 1976), pp. 30-31; Golladay and Noell, *Condition of Education,* p. 72.

72. Ibid., p. 40; NEA Research Memo, *Financial Status.*

73. *Historical Statistics of the United States: Colonial Times to 1970* (Washington: Bureau of the Census, 1975), p. 1120; *Statistical Abstract of the United States,* 1978 (Washington: Bureau of the Census), p. 260.

74. Arnold Sawislak, "Proposition 13 Voters May Be in for a Shock," *Charlottesville* (Va.) *Daily Progress,* July 20, 1978.

75. Dearman and Plisko, *Condition of Education,* p. 146; NEA Research Memo, *Financial Status,* p. 16.

76. Allan Odden and John Augenblick, *School Finance Reform in the States: 1980,* Report No. F80-1, Education Finance Center (Denver, Colorado: Education Commission of the States, April 1980), p. 23.

77. NEA Research Memo, *Teacher Supply and Demand in Public Schools,* 1978 (Washington: National Education Association, 1979).

78. Although SAT scores may be above the average at particular colleges or universities, the national average of teachers majoring in education is below those of most other college majors and has declined considerably during the late 1970s. See W. Timothy Wener, "In Search of Quality: The Need for Talent in Teaching," *Phi Delta Kappan,* September 1979, pp. 29-46; Dearborn and Plisko, *Condition of Education,* 1980, p. 132.

79. Five-year programs are now in the design or early implementation stage at a number of universities in other states, and the "Land Grant College Deans of Education" (i.e., the Association of Colleges and Schools of Education in State Universities and Land Grant Colleges) have officially endorsed the notion of extending the preservice preparation of teachers beyond the traditional four-year period.

Chapter Two

1. *Statistical Abstract of the United States,* 1979 (Washington: Bureau of the Census), pp. 313, 372.

2. "The Case of the Misplaced $30 Billion," *Business Week,* July 24, 1978, pp. 155-156.

3. *U.S. News & World Report,* June 26, 1978, p. 8.

4. NEA Research Memo, *The Status of the American Family: Policies, Facts, Opinions, and Issues* (Washington: National Education Association, 1979), p. 39.

5. *Special Analyses, Budget of the United States Government, Fiscal Year 1979,* Part 2, I, Office of the President (Washington: Government Printing Office), pp. 213-223.

6. Nancy B. Dearman and Valena White Plisko, *The Condition of Education,* 1979 Edition, Statistical Report (Washington: National Center for Education Statistics), p. 161.

7. In 1940, only 2.4% of all American women were mothers who also participated in the labor force, compared to 20.7% in 1974. A total of 11.8 (18.6%) million children are estimated to live with but one parent. See NEA Research Memo, *Status of the American Family,* p. 30.

8. "School Race Problems: The States Move In," *U.S. News & World Report,* November 28, 1977, p. 50.

9. Mary A. Golladay and Jay Noell (eds.), *The Condition of Education,* 1978 Edition, Statistical Report (Washington: National Center for Education Statistics), p. 59 reports 85.3% of whites and 50.3% of blacks oppose busing children across district lines for desegregation purposes.

10. Quoted by James M. Perry, "Is Mississippi Ready for a Black Senator? If so, It's Found Him," *Wall Street Journal,* November 2, 1978, p. 1.

11. Lorenzo Middleton, "The Effects of School Desegregation: The Debate Goes On," *Chronicle of Higher Education,* November 6, 1978. The report reviewed by Levin and Coleman was entitled *Desegregation and Black Achievement* and authored by Robert L. Crain and Rita E. Mahard of the Rand Corporation.

12. "Busing: The Issue That Will Not Go Away," *Carnegie Quarterly,* Spring, 1978.

13. Ibid.

14. *Statistical Abstract of the United States,* 1978, p. 81; Dearman and Plisko, *Condition of Education,* 1979, p. 3.

15. R. B. Zajone, "Family Configuration and Intelligence," *Science,* April 1976, pp. 227-235.

16. Quoted by Robert A. Frahm, *Racine* (Wisc.) *The Journal Times,* March 12, 1979.

17. Dorothy G. Singer and Jerome L. Singer, "Television Viewing and Aggressive Behavior in Preschool Children: A Field Study," *Forensic Psychology & Psychiatry* (New York Academy of Sciences), June 1980, pp. 289-303.

18. The April, 1978 volume of *Educational Leadership* is particularly instructive on the theme: "Youth Cultures: What We Can Learn."

19. Finding from the eighth annual Gallup Poll taken in 1976 and reported in Stanley M. Elam (ed.), *A Decade of Gallup Polls of Attitudes Toward Education,* 1969-1978 (Bloomington, Ind.: Phi Delta Kappa, 1978), p. 319.

20. Report of the Advisory Panel on the Scholastic Aptitude Test Score Decline (Willard Wirtz, chairman), *On Further Examinations* (New York: College Entrance Examination Board, 1977).

21. James Bryant Conant, *The American High School Today* (New York: McGraw-Hill, 1959).

22. W. Vance Grant and C. George Lind, *Digest of Education Statistics 1979* (Washington: National Center for Education Statistics), p. 62.

23. Roger G. Barker and Paul V. Gump, *Big School, Small School: High School Size and Student Behavior* (Stanford, Calif.: Stanford University Press, 1964).

24. Grant and Lind, *Digest,* p. 172.

25. Based on President Carter's 1981 fiscal year budget request of 13.5 billion for the Department of Education and 145.8 billion for the Department of Defense, Office of the President, *Special Analysis: Budget of the United States Government, Fiscal Year 1981* (Washington: Government Printing Office, 1980), p. 14.

26. State and local taxes provide 92 percent of the financial support for public education.

27. U.S. Office of Management and budget as cited in *U.S. News & World Report,* June 12, 1978, pp. 41-44.

28. News conference as reported in *Higher Education and National Affairs* (Washington: American Council on Education, September 16, 1977).

29. An Associated Press—NBC News poll reported by Evans Witt in the *St. Louis Globe* under the headline, "A Look at the Taxpayers Revolt Across the U.S.," June 17, 1978.

30. Organization for Economic Cooperation and Development. (Washington: *U.S. News & World Report,* December 25, 1978), p. 94. In percent of GNP spent on public education, the United States ranks in about the middle of the range of nine countries (Canada, France, Germany, Japan, Netherlands, Norway, Sweden, United Kingdom, United States), Mary A. Golladay, *The Condition of Education,* 1976 Edition (Washington: National Center for Education Statistics, 1976), pp. 267-268.

31. *Annual Report of the Commissioner of Education, Fiscal Year 1976* (Washington: Government Printing Office, 1978), pp. 236-237.

32. Grant and Lind, *Digest,* p. 93.

33. *Annual Report,* pp. 223, 236.

34. Ibid., p. 235.

35. Ibid., p. 225.

36. Ibid., p. 232.

37. Ibid., p. 224.

38. Ibid., p. 218.

39. Ibid., p. 217.

40. *Facing Up 14,* Statistical Data on Virginia's Public Schools (Richmond: Department of Education, January 1980), Table 11.

41. *Annual Report,* p. 234; Dearman and Plisko, *Condition of Education,* p. 146.

Chapter Three

1. Robert Dreeben, *On What is Learned in School* (Reading, Mass.: Addison-Wesley, 1968), pp. 67-68. Much of this section on Societal Norms draws heavily on Dreeben's concepts.

2. Ibid., p. 76.

3. In re Gault, 387 U.S. 1 (1967). This case established a "Bill of Rights" for minors.

4. Dreeben, *On What Is Learned,* p. 38.

5. Herbert H. Hyman, Charles R. Wright, and John Shelton Reed, *The Enduring Effects of Education* (Chicago: University of Chicago Press, 1975).

6. Ibid., p. 81.

7. Ibid., p. 109.

8. David E. Wiley and Annegret Harnischfeger, "Explosion of a Myth: Quantity of Schooling and Exposure to Instruction, Major Educational Vehicles," *Educational Researcher,* 3, April 1974, p. 9.

9. Annegret Harnischfeger and David E. Wiley, "The Marrow of Achievement Test Score Declines," *Educational Technology,* June 1976, pp. 5-14.

10. Donald M. Medley, *Teacher Competence and Teacher Effectiveness: A Review of Process-Product Research* (Washington: American Associaiton of Colleges for Teacher Education, August 1977).

11. Stanley M. Elam (ed.), *A Decade of Gallup Polls of Attitudes Toward Education, 1969-1978* (Bloomington, Ind.: Phi Delta Kappa, 1978), p. 299.

12. *Improving Educational Achievement,* Report of the National Academy of Education Committee on Testing and Basic Skills to the Assistant Secretary for Education(Washington: National Academy of Education, March 1978), p. 3.

13. Ibid.

14. David Berliner, " 'Time on Task' Makes a Big Difference in Learning, and There's the Rub," *Phi Delta Kappan,* January 1979, p. 338.

15. Benjamin S. Bloom, *Human Characteristics and School Learning* (New York: McGraw-Hill, 1976).

16. *Improving Educational Achievement,* p. 6.

17. Similar conclusions are reached by others. See, for example, Harold Hodgkinson, "What's Right with Education," *Phi Delta Kappan,* 61, November 1979, pp. 159-162.

18. One particularly useful document reviewing the relationship between education and work is Barry E. Stern, *Toward a Federal Policy on Education and Work* (Washington: U.S. Department of Health, Education and Welfare, Government Printing Office, March 1977).

19. The three components of the hidden curriculum, described in the following pages, are thoroughly discussed in Philip W. Jackson, *Life in Classrooms* (New York: Holt, Rinehart and Winston, 1968).

20. W. Vance Grant and C. George Lind, *Digest of Education Statistics 1979,* (Washington: National Center for Education Statistics), pp. 191-192.

21. Nancy B. Dearman and Valena White Plisko, *The Condition of Education,* 1979 Edition (Washington: National Center for Education Statistics), p. 205.

22. Gordon I. Swanson, "Vocational Education: Fact and Fantasy," *Phi Delta Kappan,* 60, October 1978, pp. 87-90.

23. Diane Ravitch, *The Revisionists Revised: A Critique on the Radical Attack on the Schools* (New York: Basic Books, 1977), p. 110.

24. Bloom, *Human Characteristics,* p. 167.

25. Ibid., p. 171.

26. Jane A. Stallings, "What Teachers Do Does Make a Difference—A Study of Seven Follow Through Educational Models," in Allen B. Calvin (ed.), *Perspectives on Education* (Reading, Mass.: Addison-Wesley, 1977), pp. 49-65.

27. Medley, *Teacher Competence;* N. L. Gage, *The Scientific Basis of the Art of Teaching* (New York: Teachers College Press, Columbia University, 1977); Penelope L. Peterson and Herbert J. Walberg (eds.) *Research on Teaching: Concepts, Findings and Implications* (Berkeley, Calif.: McCutchan, 1979).

28. Stallings, *What Teachers Do Does Make a Difference.*

29. Medley, *Teacher Competence,* p. 18. Some experts would argue against using student achievement gains as a measure of teacher effectiveness. Some would also question the use of the term effective teachers, given the current state of research knowledge.

30. Ibid., pp. 16-18.

31. Ibid.

32. Ibid., Table 38.

33. G. John Berclay (ed.), *Parent Involvement in the Schools* (Washington: National Education Association, 1977).

34. Jane Stallings, Margaret Needels, and Nicholas Stayrook, *How to Change the Process of Teaching Basic Reading Skills in Secondary Schools: Phase II and Phase III,* Final Report (Palo Alto, Calif.: SRI International, 1979).

35. Ibid., p. xx.

36. Jeanne S. Park (ed.), *Education in Action: 50 Ideas that Work* (Washington: U. S. Department Of Health, Education and Welfare, Government Printing Office, 1978).

37. Same references and notations as in Note 36 (Chapter 1) above.

38. Bloom, *Human Characteristics,* p. 71.

39. Nancy B. Dearman and Valena White Plisko, *The Condition of Education,* 1980 Edition (Washington: National Center for Education Statistics), p. 24.

40. Bernard A. Faller, Jr., "The Basics: How Far Is Back?" *Phi Delta Kappan,* 60, January 1979, pp. 375-376.

41. Charles Gadway and H. A. Wilson, *Functional Literacy: Basic Reading Performance* (Denver Colo.: National Assessment of Educational Progress, 1976).

42. Sar A. Levitan, William B. Johnston, and Robert Taggart, "The Impact of Schooling on American Blacks," in Arthur J. Newman (ed.), *In Defense of the American Public School* (Cambridge, Mass.: Schenkman Publishing, 1978), pp. 129-137.

43. Ravitch, *Revisionists Revised,* p. 112.

44. "What's Right with U.S. Schools," *Parade,* April 19, 1964.

45. "Is Russia's School System So Good After All?" *U.S. News & World Report,* February 3, 1964, pp. 70-71.

46. Ibid.

47. Grace and Fred Hechinger, "Are Schools Better in Other Countries?" *American Education,* 10, January-February 1974, pp. 6-8.

48. Ralph W. Tyler, "The U.S. vs. the World: A Comparison of Educational Performance," *Phi Delta Kappan,* 62, January, 1981, pp. 307-310.

49. Thomas F. Donlon and Gary J. Echternacht, *A Feasibility Study of the SAT Performance of High-Ability Students From 1960 to 1974* (Valedictorian Study) (Princeton, N.J.: College Entrance Examination Board, February 1977).

50. Tyler, Ibid., p. 308.

Chapter Four

1. W. Vance Grant and C. George Lind, *Digest of Education Statistics 1979* (Washington: National Center for Education Statistics), p. 23.

2. Nancy B. Dearman and Valena White Plisko, *The Condition of Education,* 1980 Edition, Statistical Report (Washington: National Center for Education Statistics), p. 40.

3. "Help! Teacher Can't Teach!" *Time,* June 16, 1980, pp. 54-63.

4. U.S. Department of Health, Education and Welfare, Office of Civil Rights, *Final Title IX Regulations Implementing Education Amendments of 1972 Prohibiting Sex Discrimination in Education* (Washington: Government Printing Office, 1975).

5. Recent studies of how time is spent in elementary classrooms indicate that an average of 55-60% of school time is allocated to academic activities (reading, mathematics, science, and social studies). The remaining time is devoted to nonacademic subjects (art, music, story-telling, sharing, physical education) and noninstructional activities (waiting between activities, transitions, class business). Classes vary considerably, however, with some spending an hour per day more than others on academic subjects. See Carolyn Denham and Ann Lieberman (eds.), *Time to Learn* (Washington: National Institute for Education, May 1980).

6. "Education for Minorities Has Improved," *Report on Education Research* (Washington: Capitol Publications, November 1, 1978), p. 9.

7. Patricia A. Graham in *Reflections and Recommendations,* Fourth Annual Report of the National Council on Educational Research (Washington: National Institute of Education, 1978), p. 18. For a similar statement see *Improving Educational Achievements,* Report of the National Academy of Education, Committee on Testing and Basic Skills, to the Assistant Secretary of Education, March 1978.

8. Paul Berman and Milbrey Wallin McLaughlin, *Federal Programs Supporting Educational Change,* vol. VIII: Implementing and Sustaining Innovations (Santa Monica, Calif.: Rand Corporation, May 1978), p. vi.

9. Gail McCutcheon, "How Do Elementary School Teachers Plan? The Nature of Planning and Influences on It," *Elementary School Journal,* 81, September 1980, pp. 4-23.

10. Lewis Lyman, "The National School Lunch Program: Boon or Boondoggle?" *Phi Delta Kappan,* 60, February 1979, pp. 436-438.

11. William C. Miller, "Unobtrusive Measures Can Help in Assessing Growth," *Educational Leadership,* 35, January 1978, pp. 264-269.

12. William M. Bulkeley, "Some School Systems Use Business Methods to Make Pupils Learn," *Wall Street Journal,* May 30, 1978.

13. Dearman and Plisko, *Condition of Education,* p. 54.

14. "A Social Strategy Aimed at Profits," *Business Week,* June 25, 1979, p. 118.

15. *Business Week,* September 11, 1978, p. 130.

16. "Labor Dept. Grants $3.3 Million To Employ Dropouts," *Charlottesville* (Va.) *Daily Progress,* March 10, 1979.

17. *Reflections and Recommendations,* p. 27.

18. Edward B. Fiske, "Job Training Schools Grow Along with Cries of Abuses " (July 25, 1979), "Who Enrolls and Why" (July 26, 1979), and "State Seeks Tighter Control of Vocational Education" (July 27, 1979), *New York Times.*

19. Evans Clinchy and Elizabeth Allen Cody, "If Not Public Choice, Then Private Escape," *Phi Delta Kappan,* 59, December 1978, pp. 270-273.

20. Ibid.

21. Robert T. Greene, Cornelia Belsches and Maria Mladenoff, "Richmond's Progressive Solution to Declining High School Enrollments," *Phi Delta Kappan,* 61, May 1980, pp. 616-617.

22. Clinchy and Cody, "If Not Public Choice," p. 271.

23. Vernon H. Smith, "Optional Alternative Public Schools," in Arthur J. Newman (ed.), *In Defense of the American Public School* (Cambridge, Mass.: Schenkman Publishing, 1978), p. 175.

24. David G. Savage, "Wingate: Brooklyn's Born-Again High School," *Educational Leadership,* 36, May 1979, pp. 541-545. According to recent Gallup Poll findings more than 8 out of 10 persons favor the Wingate approach, i.e., requiring non-English speaking children to learn the language before being taught other subjects rather than being enrolled in bilingual programs and exposed to various subjects in their native language until they learn English. See George H. Gallup, "The 12th Annual Gallup Poll of the Public's Attitudes Toward the Public Schools," *Phi Delta Kappan,* 62, September 1980, p. 44.

25. Wilbur Brookover et al., *School Systems and School Achievement* (Brooklyn, N.Y.: J.F. Bergin, 1979); David L. Clark, Linda S. Motto, and Martha M. McCarthy, "Factors Associated with Success in Urban Elementary Schools," *Phi Delta Kappan,* 61, March 1980, pp. 467-470; Ronald R. Edmonds, "Some Schools Work and More Can," *Social Policy,* 9, March/April 1979, pp. 28-32; Ronald Edmonds, "Effective Schools for the Urban Poor," *Educational Leadership,* 37, October 1979, pp. 15-24; see also a critique of the latter research by Ralph Scott and Herbert J. Walberg, "Schools Alone Are Insufficient: A Response to Edmonds," *Educational Leadership,* 37, October 1979, pp. 24-27.

26. "Hartford's Workplaces Become the Classroom," *Business Week,* December 5, 1977, pp. 117-118.

27. Eliot Wigginton, "Introduction—Foxfire 6," in Committee on Education and Labor, House of Representatives, Ninety-Sixth Congress, *Needs of Elementary and Secondary Education in the 1980's,* (Washington: Government Printing Office, 1980), p. 439.

28. John I. Goodlad, *What Schools Are For* (Bloomington, Ind.: Phi Delta Kappa Educational Foundation, 1979), p. 120.

29. Thomas J. Burns, Chairman, *The Urban High School Reform Initiative,* Final Report (Washington: U. S. Department of Health, Education and Welfare, Office of Education, September 1979), p. 42.

30. James S. Coleman et al., *Equality of Educational Opportunity* (Washington: Government Printing Office, 1966).

31. G. John Berclay (ed.), *Parent Involvement In the Schools* (Washington: National Education Association, 1977).

32. Ernest L. Boyer, "Quality and the Campus: The High School/College Connection," *AAHE Bulletin,* May 1980, p. 11.

33. Paul C. Berg, "Who Is Literate?" *Compact,* Summer 1979, pp. 11-13.

34. Ibid.

35. *Science and Engineering Education for the 1980s and Beyond.* Report to the President of the United States by the National Science Foundation and the Department of Education, October 1980, p. 144.

36. Ibid., p. 137.

37. Irving H. Buchen, "Curriculum 2000: Futures Basics," in Committee on Education and Labor, *Needs in the 1980's,* p. 392.

38. Benjamin H. Alexander,"Black English: A Modern Version of Paternalism," *Chronicle of Higher Education,* May 27, 1980, p. 21.

39. James Block and Lorin Anderson, *Mastery Learning in Classroom Instruction* (New York: Macmillan, 1975).

40. Joan S. Hyman and S. Alan Cohen, "Learning for Mastery: Ten Conclusions After 15 Years and 3,000 Schools," *Educational Leadership,* 37, November 1979, p. 109.

41. Herbert J. Walberg, Diane Schiller, and Geneva D. Haertel, "The Quiet Revolution in Educational Research," *Phi Delta Kappan,* 61, November 1979, pp. 179-183.

42. Liz Roman Gallese, "Computers Find Wider Use in Classrooms As Small Machines Help to Lower Costs," *Wall Street Journal,* June 3, 1980, p. 48.

43. Ibid.

44. Walberg, Schiller, and Haertel, "Quiet Revolution," also "Computers Are Fun, But Can They Teach?" *ETS Developments* (Princeton, N.J.: Educational Testing Service, Winter 1979), pp. 1-2.

45. Same references as in Note 25 (Chapter 4) above.

46. Virginia State Department of Education, "Preliminary Proposal for a Career Teacher Certificate," Richmond, Virginia, 1979 (Mimeographed.)

47. Included in the 1980 resolutions of the National Education Association are the following statements: "The Association opposes any plan to rank teachers on the basis of competency." "The Association believes that instructional performance pay schedules, such as merit pay, are inappropriate because of the complexity of the teaching-learning process." Both statements have been endorsed officially by the organization for several years.

48. *U.S. News & World Report*, May 12, 1980, p. 52.

49. William F. Casey, III, "Would Bear Bryant Teach in the Public Schools? The Need for Teacher Incentives," *Phi Delta Kappan*, 60, March 1979, pp. 500-501.

50. Dan C. Lortie, *Schoolteacher: A Sociological Study* (Chicago: University of Chicago Press, 1975), p. 10.

51. Dearman and Plisko, *Condition of Education*, p. 146.

52. Alfonso A. Narvaez, "Newark School Board Will Discharge 1,723 and Eliminate 'Frills'," *New York Times*, December 9, 1978; Thomas W. Lippman, "D. C. Schools' 1982 Funds Are Reduced," *Washington Post*, August 5, 1980.

53. "Over time, capital-intensive industries cost consumers progressively less, relative to labor-intensive industries, because salaries rise faster than capital costs. (For example, from 1965 to 1975 the Consumer Price Index rose 69%; educational costs rose 155%)" from Chris Dede, "The Next Ten Years in Education," in Committee on Education and Labor, *Needs in the 1980's*, p. 392.

54. Walberg, Schiller, and Haertel, "Quiet Revolution."

55. Carl D. Perkins, "States Count in ESEA Amendments," *Compact*, Summer 1979, p. 8.

56. "Judge Bans Use of IQ Tests for Placement; Calls Them Racially Biased," *Phi Delta Kappan*, 61, December 1979, p. 295.

57. Thomas J. Flygare, "Detecting Drugs in School: The Legality of Scent Dogs and Strip Searches," *Phi Delta Kappan*, 61, December 1979, pp. 280-281.

58. Elaine Yaffe, "Public Education: Society's Band-Aid," *Phi Delta Kappan*, 61, March 1980, p. 452.

59. "Help! Teacher Can't Teach!" *Time*, June 16, 1980, p. 59.

60. Elizabeth A. Dillon-Peterson, "Position Paper," in Committee on Education and Labor, *Needs in the 1980's*, p. 369.

61. Leonard P. Stavisky, "Dilemma for Decision Makers: Contradictory Education Research," *Compact*, Summer 1979, pp. 24-26.

62. Daniel Linden Duke, Irene Muzio, "How Effective Are Alternative Schools? A Review of Recent Evaluations and Reports," *Teachers College Record*, 79, February 1978, pp. 461-483.

63. William Greider, "Stop Knocking Our Schools," *Washington Post*, June 3, 1979.

64. Allan Odden and John Augenblick, *School Finance Reform in the States: 1980*, Report No. F80-1, Education Finance Center (Denver, Colorado: Education Commission of the States, April 1980), p. 21.

65. Owen B. Kiernan, in Committee on Education and Labor, *Needs in the 1980's*, p. 145; also in the 12th Annual Gallup Poll of public attitudes toward public schools, more confidence was indicated toward the schools than toward the courts, local government, state government, national government, labor unions or big business. Only the churches ranked higher. See George H. Gallup, *Phi Delta Kappan*, 62, September 1980, p. 35.

66. Dearman and Plisko, *Condition of Education*, pp. 70-71.

67. "Interview with Author James Michener," *U. S. News & World Report*, February 4, 1980, p. 42.

68. "A Conversation with Amitai Etzioni," *U. S. News & World Report*, April 14, 1980, p. 54.

ABOUT THE AUTHOR

Richard Brandt's career in education spans more than three decades. He has taught in the public schools in Michigan, his home state, and served on the faculties of three universities. After completing his doctorate at the University of Maryland in 1954, he remained on the faculty of that institution in its Institute for Child Study teaching courses in human development and serving as consultant to school systems throughout the country. He joined the faculty of the School of Education at the University of Virginia in 1965, becoming Chairman of its Foundations of Education Department in 1968 and Dean in 1974.

Author of several dozen professional articles, chapters, reviews, and monographs, his book *Studying Behavior in Natural Settings* (Holt, Rinehart and Winston, 1972) was one of the first comprehensive texts on naturalistic research. His interest in the present topic stems primarily from serving as advisor to school administrators and becoming sensitive to the vast array of problems they face at a time when public education is undergoing tremendous criticism and change. This book is his attempt to address that criticism by reassessing what our schools have accomplished and indicating changes that must be made if those problems are to be resolved.